2.50

CW00385828

We all lead such busy lives these days.
Perhaps it's your time-consuming job, or the demands that
come with a young family. No matter what, this cookbook is
just the solution you've been looking for.
We believe that this is the first-ever cookbook entirely
consisting of recipes with *no more than six ingredients* — and
there are dozens of them!
This cuts down on your shopping time, simplifies your cooking,
and leaves you more precious time to spend with the people
you care for.
All the recipes in this book are fresh, easy to prepare and
delicious. They really do prove that 'Cooking Can Be Simple'.
We've included a helpful list of Store Cupboard ingredients on
page 48; this will improve your shopping time even more.
P.S. If you think we've cheated about 'Six-Ingredients-Only' by
omitting salt and pepper, remember not everyone likes to
season food. Simply add these to your taste.
Good cooking!

Editor Philip Gore **Designer** Craig Osment **Art Director** Stephen Joseph **Cookery Editor** Loukie Werle **Food Stylist** Wendy Berecry **Home Economist** Belinda Warn **Editorial Production** Margaret Gore & Associates **Photography** Warren Webb **Typesetting** APT **Printed** in Japan by Dai Nippon, Tokyo
Published by Century Magazines Pty Ltd, 216-224 Commonwealth Street, Surry Hills, NSW 2010, Australia. Tel: (02) 281 3544 **UK Distribution** T.B. Clarke (UK) Distributors Ltd, Beckett House, 14 Billing Road, Northampton NN1 5AW. Tel: (0604) 23 0941. Fax: (0604) 23 0942. **Australian Distribution** (Supermarkets) Select Magazines Pty Ltd, Suite 402, 7 Merriwa Street, Gordon, NSW 2072. (Newsagents) NDD 150 Bourke Road, Alexandria, NSW 2015. ©Century Magazines Pty Ltd. *Recommended retail price.
Photography credits We gratefully acknowledge the following suppliers: **Accoutrement,** Mosman; **Australian East India Company,** Darlinghurst and Bondi Junction; **Keyhole Cane,** Neutral Bay; **The Design Store,** Mosman; **Villa Italiana,** Darlinghurst; **Hale Importers,** Brookvale; **Villeroy & Boch,** Brookvale; **Pazotti Tiles,** Woollahra; **Opus,** Paddington.

SIMPLE SOUPS

Served hot or cold these delicious soups are easy to make and are ideal for family meals or entertaining.

Avocado Summer Soup

4 ripe avocados, peeled and stoned

2 cups chicken stock

½ cup cream

¼ cup dry white wine

3 tblspn lemon juice

1 Chop avocado flesh and puree in processor or blender.

2 While motor is running add stock, cream, wine and lemon juice, blend until smooth.

3 Chill soup until ready to serve. Garnish as desired.

Serves 4 to 6

Chilled Spinach Soup with Sour Cream

1 onion, chopped

60g (2oz) unsalted butter

1 tblspn flour

2½ cups chicken stock

500g (1lb) cooked spinach, chopped

450ml (¾ pint) sour cream

1 Cook onion in butter until soft, about 5 minutes. Add flour, cook 2 minutes, stirring constantly.

2 Gradually add stock, stirring constantly, cook until mixture thickens.

3 Add spinach, season to taste with salt and freshly ground pepper, cook 5 minutes. Puree in a food processor, add 300ml (½ pint) sour cream, blend well.

4 Pour into a serving dish, allow to cool, cover and refrigerate at least 4 hours or overnight.

5 When ready to serve correct seasoning, ladle soup into bowls, swirl in remaining sour cream to garnish.

Serves 6

Chilled Melon and Cucumber Soup

1 rockmelon, peeled and seeded

4 cucumbers, peeled and seeded

2 tblspn honey

2 tblspn lemon juice

8-12 sprigs of mint

1 In a food processor or blender, puree rockmelon and cucumber until smooth; strain.

2 Add the honey and lemon juice; pour mixture into jug, cover and set aside.

3 Roughly cut mint (reserve some for garnish) and mix into puree mixture. Let mixture stand for 5 hours at room temperature.

4 Remove mint from soup, chill until ready to serve.

Serves 4 to 6

*Avocado Summer Soup (top);
Chilled Melon and Cucumber Soup*

Italian Cauliflower Soup

125g (4oz) unsalted butter

1 small onion, chopped

6 cups chicken stock

1 cauliflower, divided into flowerets

1 cup Arborio rice

1/3 cup Parmesan cheese

1 Melt 90g (3oz) butter in a saucepan. Add onion, saute until golden brown.

2 Add stock, cauliflower and rice. Season to taste with salt and freshly ground pepper. Bring to a boil and cook uncovered for 20 minutes.

3 While still over heat, stir in remaining butter and Parmesan cheese. Serve immediately.

Serves 6

Carrot Soup with Basil Cream

1 onion, finely chopped

45g (1½oz) unsalted butter

1.25kg (2½lb) carrots, peeled, coarsely chopped

about 8 cups chicken stock

½ cup cream

3 tblspn chopped basil

1 Gently cook onion in butter until soft. Add carrots, mix well. Cook 10 minutes, stirring occasionally.

2 Add just enough stock to cover the carrots, simmer until tender. Puree mixture in a mouli, add more stock to obtain the right consistency. Season to taste with salt and freshly ground pepper.

3 Allow to cool, cover and refrigerate at least 4 hours or overnight.

4 Whip cream, fold in chopped basil. Season to taste with salt. Ladle chilled soup into bowls, float dollops of basil cream on top.

Serves 8

Chestnut Soup

125g (4oz) unsalted butter

1 onion, coarsely chopped

2 carrots, coarsely chopped

¼ cup plain flour

8 cups chicken stock

500g (1lb) canned chestnuts, or fresh chestnuts, cooked

1 Melt butter in a saucepan, add onions and carrots, cook gently until light golden and soft, about 5 minutes.

2 Add flour, stir to coat vegetables, cook gently for 3 minutes, stirring constantly.

3 Add chicken stock gradually. Add chestnuts, season to taste with salt and freshly ground black pepper. Simmer soup uncovered for 30 minutes.

4 Puree soup in a food processor until smooth. Reheat and if desired, add 1 cup cream. This will make the soup richer, but will considerably detract from the chestnut flavour. Serve hot.

Serves 8

Cucumber Soup with Prawns (Shrimp)

3 medium cucumbers

1/3 cup dill sprigs

1 cup buttermilk

1 cup sour cream

1 large clove garlic

125g (4oz) cooked prawns (shrimp)

1 Peel cucumbers, slice ½ a cucumber very thinly, set aside for garnish. Chop remaining cucumbers roughly. Set aside 4 dill sprigs for garnish.

2 Combine cucumber, buttermilk, sour cream, garlic and remaining dill in a food processor. Puree until smooth. Pour into a bowl, cover, refrigerate at least 2 hours or overnight.

3 When ready to serve, ladle soup into bowls, garnish with prawns, cucumber slices and sprigs of dill.

Serves 4

Chilled Coriander Yoghurt Soup

3 x 200ml (6½oz) cartons plain yoghurt

2 cups chopped fresh coriander

½ cup finely chopped onion

1 cup cream

3 cups chicken stock

1 In a food processor or blender, puree yoghurt, coriander, onion and cream until smooth.

2 Pour into a large container, add stock, mix well.

3 Chill until ready to serve. Garnish as desired.

Serves 4 to 6

Cream of Corn and Red Capsicum (Pepper) Soup

2 red capsicum (pepper)

2 tspn arrowroot

2 onions, peeled and chopped

2 cups chicken stock

3 cups corn kernels

1 cup cream

1 Roast capsicum over an open flame until charred all over, about 5 minutes. Seal the capsicum in a paper bag and 'sweat' for 10 minutes. Rub charred skin off and rinse. Pat dry and remove seeds and stems, puree in a blender until smooth; strain.

2 Heat puree in small saucepan until boiling. Combine arrowroot with 3 tablespoons of capsicum puree, mix to a paste; mix into boiling puree mixture, remove from heat.

3 In a large saucepan combine onions and stock, cook 5 minutes. Add corn, cook a further 10 minutes.

4 Puree soup in blender or processor, return to saucepan. Add cream. Serve soup hot and decorate with a swirl of capsicum puree.

Serves 4

Italian Fettucine Consomme

3 cloves garlic, crushed

½ cup chopped tinned tomatoes

1 cup chicken stock

350g (11oz) fresh fettucine

2 tblspn fresh basil, chopped

1 cup fresh Parmesan cheese, grated

1 In a large saucepan place 3 tablespoons water, heat; add garlic and 'sweat' until water has evaporated.

2 Add tomatoes and 3 cups of water, add stock and bring to the boil.

3 Add fettucine and cook until al dente; about 7 minutes.

4 Remove from heat, stir in half the basil and half the cheese. Decorate each serve with remaining basil and cheese.

Serves 6

Chilled Coriander Yoghurt Soup (top); Cream of Corn and Red Capsicum (Pepper) Soup

Quick Tomato Soup with Avocado

500g (1lb) tomatoes, peeled, chopped

1 large red capsicum (pepper), peeled, seeded, chopped

½ cup cream

¼ tspn Tabasco sauce

½ avocado, cut into ½cm (¼in) cubes

1 Puree tomatoes and pepper in a food processor. Add cream and Tabasco, blend well. Season to taste with salt.

2 Pour into a serving bowl, cover, refrigerate at least 2 hours or overnight. Serve sprinkled with avocado.

Serves 4

Italian Fettucine Consomme

Cold Cherry Soup

1 cup castor sugar

4 cups pitted sour cherries, drained

¼ cup orange juice

1 tblspn arrowroot

½ cup dry red wine

½ cup cream

1 In a large saucepan combine 3 cups of water with castor sugar, bring mixture to the boil, carefully stirring and washing down any sugar crystals from the side of the saucepan with a brush dipped in cold water.

2 Boil syrup for 5 minutes, add cherries and simmer 30 minutes.

3 In a small jug, combine orange juice and arrowroot until smooth. Pour into cherry mixture, stir, simmer further 5 minutes.

4 Remove from heat and cool. Chill before serving; stir in wine, decorate with cream, or as desired.

Serves 4

Spinach Soup with Garlic

5 cloves garlic, crushed

6 rashers of bacon, chopped

5 cups chicken stock

2 packets frozen spinach or 2 cups cooked spinach

½ cup sour cream

½ tspn nutmeg

1 Place crushed garlic in large saucepan with bacon, cook over low heat 5 minutes, or until bacon becomes transparent.

2 Add stock, bring to a boil, reduce heat and simmer 10 minutes; add spinach, simmer further 10 minutes.

3 Process or blend mixture until smooth, add sour cream and nutmeg. Serve immediately. Garnish as desired.

Serves 6

Cold Cherry Soup (top); Spinach Soup with Garlic

Curly Endive Soup

1 large head curly endive

250g (½lb) vermicelli

¼ cup olive oil

2 eggs, beaten

Parmesan cheese

1 Wash endive in several changes cold water. Cut into strips. In a saucepan bring 8 cups of lightly salted water to a boil, add endive and cook, covered, until tender, about 7 minutes.

2 Remove endive with a slotted spoon, set aside.

3 Add vermicelli to boiling endive water, stir until water returns to the boil. Cook until just tender, about 6 minutes.

4 Reduce heat to a simmer, return endive to saucepan. Add olive oil and season to taste with salt and freshly ground black pepper.

5 Pour the beaten eggs slowly into the pan while stirring. The egg will form fine ribbons. Serve hot, pass a bowl of Parmesan cheese separately.

Serves 8

Pear and Celery Soup

125g (4oz) unsalted butter

1 large onion, coarsely chopped

6 stalks celery, coarsely chopped

6 cups chicken stock

750g (1½lb) pears, peeled, cored, chopped

½ cup cream

1 Melt butter in a saucepan. Add onion, cook until light golden, about 15 minutes.

2 Add celery, cover and cook gently until celery is tender, about 15 minutes, stirring from time to time.

3 Add stock, bring to a boil, reduce heat to medium, cook covered 30 minutes, stirring occasionally.

Cream of Squash Soup

4 Add pears, reduce heat to a simmer, cook until pears are tender, about 20 minutes. Stir occasionally. Allow soup to cool slightly.

5 Puree soup in a food processor. Sieve back into the saucepan. Add cream, reheat to a simmer over gentle heat, stirring constantly. Season to taste with salt and freshly ground pepper. Serve hot, garnished with a little chopped parsley, if desired.

Serves 6

Spring Onion (Scallion) Soup

8 bunches spring onions (scallions)
125g (4oz) unsalted butter
1 Granny Smith apple, peeled, cored, coarsely chopped
2 large cloves garlic, coarsely chopped
6 cups chicken stock
½ cup sour cream

1 Coarsely chop 6 bunches of spring onions, reserve 2 bunches. Melt butter in a saucepan, add spring onions, apple and garlic. Stir-fry until soft and golden, about 5 minutes.

2 Add chicken stock, bring to a boil. Reduce heat and simmer uncovered, for 30 minutes.

3 Pour soup into a food processor and puree. Sieve back into the saucepan. Season to taste with salt and freshly ground pepper.

4 Slice remaining 2 bunches of spring onions into thin rings. Add to soup, reserving about ¼ cup for garnish.

5 Bring soup to a boil. Ladle into soup bowls, serve with a dollop of sour cream and garnish with reserved spring onions.

Serves 6

Cream of Squash Soup

500g (1lb) yellow squash, chopped
1 tblspn butter
1 onion, chopped
2 cups chicken stock
1 cup sour cream
pinch nutmeg

1 Melt butter in a large saucepan, add squash and onion, cook over moderate heat until squash is cooked through.

2 Add stock to mixture, bring to the boil and simmer 20 minutes, or until squash falls apart.

3 Remove from heat and puree mixture in a food processor or blender until smooth.

4 Transfer mixture into a large saucepan, mix in cream and nutmeg, season to taste. Re-heat and serve immediately. Garnish as desired.

Serves 4

PERFECT STARTERS

These dishes have been designed to stimulate the tastebuds. Their unique combination of flavours make them ideal, appetising first courses.

Warm Mussel Salad with Walnut Dressing

assorted lettuce leaves
small bunch watercress
1½ cups dry white wine
½ cup chopped spring onions (scallions)
16 mussels, scrubbed and debearded
¼ cup walnut oil

1 Wash and dry lettuce leaves, arrange decoratively with watercress on serving plate.

2 Bring wine to the boil in medium saucepan, add spring onions and ½ cup water. Add mussels, cook until shells open.

3 Remove from saucepan, reserving liquid. Remove top shell from each mussel and place mussels on the lettuce and watercress bed.

4 Mix 4 tablespoons of the reserved liquid with walnut oil, use to dress the salad. Garnish with walnut pieces if desired.

Serves 4

Asparagus with Parmesan Cheese and Prosciutto

1kg (2lb) asparagus, trimmed, peeled
¼ cup unsalted butter
¼ cup freshly grated Parmesan cheese
60g (2oz) thinly sliced prosciutto, cut into matchsticks

1 Cook asparagus in lightly salted boiling water until barely tender but still crisp, about 7 minutes. Drain. Rinse under cold running water. Drain, pat dry with paper towels. Place in a gratin dish.

2 Melt butter, pour over asparagus, season to taste with salt and freshly ground pepper. Toss well to coat, sprinkle with cheese.

3 Place dish under a grill until cheese is bubbling. Sprinkle with prosciutto. Serve hot.

Serves 6

Hot Crabmeat Gratin

500g (1lb) cooked crabmeat
3 thick slices bacon, cut in half
1½ cup mayonnaise
½ cup chilli sauce
1 tspn hot mustard powder
½ tspn Tabasco sauce

1 Divide crabmeat between 6 buttered ovenproof dishes. Cover with foil and heat in a hot oven for 5 minutes. Remove from oven, discard foil.

2 Cook bacon slices in a frying pan until crisp. Place on top of crabmeat.

3 In a bowl combine mayonnaise, chilli sauce, mustard powder and Tabasco. Pour over crabmeat dishes. Place under a grill until top is bubbling. Serve hot.

Serves 6

Warm Mussel Salad with Walnut Dressing

Oven-baked Avocados

2 avocados

⅓ cup mayonnaise

pinch of curry powder

¼ tspn Tabasco sauce

1 large egg white

watercress

1 Halve avocados, remove pips and peel carefully. Cut a very thin slice off the bottom so avocados will sit firmly.

2 In a small bowl combine mayonnaise with curry powder and Tabasco. Season with salt and freshly ground pepper if necessary.

3 In another bowl beat egg white until stiff, fold gently but thoroughly into mayonnaise mixture.

4 Divide mixture between avocado halves, bake in a 180°C (350°F) oven until filling is golden. Serve hot, garnish plates with watercress.

Serves 4

Smoked Salmon Mousse

1 tblspn olive oil

250g (½lb) Atlantic salmon fillet

1 tblspn brandy

250g (½lb) smoked salmon

375ml (12 fl oz) cream

1 tblspn pink peppercorns, drained

1 Slice salmon fillet into ½cm (¼in) thick slices, cut slices into 2½ x ½cm (1 x ¼in) strips.

2 Warm oil gently in a frying pan, add salmon strips and saute until fish is opaque, about 3 minutes.

3 Add brandy, ignite. When flames have died down, remove salmon and pan juices to a plate. Allow to cool, refrigerate until barely chilled, about 15 minutes.

4 Cut smoked salmon into medium pieces, combine in a food processor with 1 cup of the cream. Add freshly grated black pepper to taste. Puree until smooth.

5 In a large bowl combine fresh salmon with the smoked salmon mixture and pink peppercorns.

6 Beat remaining cream until stiff, fold half thoroughly into salmon mixture to incorporate, lightly fold in remaining cream.

7 Spoon into a terrine or serving dish, cover, refrigerate overnight. Serve cold with toast or crackers.

Serves 8

Artichoke Hearts Stuffed with Two Cheeses

500g (1lb) jar artichoke hearts, drained

3 tblspn ricotta cheese

2 tblspn grated Parmesan cheese

1 tblspn finely chopped red capsicum (pepper)

1 tspn finely chopped parsley

¼ tspn black cracked pepper

1 Slice bottoms off artichoke hearts so they will stand upright.

2 In a small bowl, combine ricotta, Parmesan, capsicum, parsley and pepper; mix well.

3 Spoon mixture into the centre of each heart and grill for 1 minute or until the cheese begins to turn golden.

Serves 4

Pear and Prosciutto with Cream Cheese

155g (5oz) soft cream cheese

juice of 1 lemon

90g (3oz) prosciutto, cut into thin strips

4 spring onions (scallions), chopped

4 small pears, peeled and cored

watercress

1 Place cream cheese and lemon juice in a food processor. Blend until smooth. Remove from processor, add prosciutto and spring onions. Mix well.

Artichoke Hearts Stuffed with Two Cheeses

2 Mound cheese mixture onto 4 small plates. Cut pears into neat slices, arrange on plates, decorate with sprigs of watercress.

Serves 4

Creamy Oyster Dip

24 oysters, removed from shells

½ cup cream

¼ cup milk

½ cup sour cream

2 tblspn tomato sauce

¼ tspn potato flour

1 Rinse oysters and place in a small bowl, cover and refrigerate.

2 In a small saucepan, over medium heat, combine cream, milk, sour cream, tomato sauce and potato flour. Slowly bring to the boil, stirring constantly until mixture thickens.

3 Remove from heat and stir in oysters. Serve with hot toast or biscuits.

Serves 4

Smoked Chicken with Orange and Mango Salad

1 smoked chicken, about 1.25kg (2½lb)

1 orange, peeled, segmented

1 mango, sliced

1 head witlof (UK chicory, US Belgian endive), leaves separated

½ cup vinaigrette

¼ cup freshly squeezed orange juice

1 Slice chicken into neat slices.

2 Arrange witlof leaves, orange and mango on 4 plates. Top with chicken.

3 Combine vinaigrette and orange juice in a screwtop jar. Shake until well combined. Pour over salad, serve immediately.

Serves 4

Creamy Oyster Dip

Cold Poached Prawns (Shrimp) in Pernod

250g (½lb) medium green prawns (shrimp)

3 tblspn oil

¼ cup pernod

1 bunch asparagus, cut in half

1 tblspn parsley, chopped

2 tblspn lime juice

1 Shell and devein prawns, leaving tails intact.

2 In a large frying pan, heat oil and pernod over moderate heat. Add asparagus, cook for 1 minute. Remove asparagus with a slotted spoon.

3 Add prawns to frying pan and cook for 2 minutes; remove with slotted spoon.

4 Decoratively arrange asparagus and prawns on a serving plate.

5 Add lime juice and parsley to the pan juices, pour over prawns and asparagus, add pepper to taste if desired.

Serves 2-3

Fish Mousseline with Cream Sauce

250g (½lb) smoked cod fish fillets

250g (½lb) green prawns (shrimp), shelled and deveined

2 egg whites

1 cup cream plus 1 cup cream extra

⅓ cup dry white wine

2 tblspn spring onions (scallions), finely chopped

1 Cut fish and prawns into 2cm (¾in) pieces and process in a blender until smooth. Add egg whites one at a time and process until combined.

2 While the blender is operating pour in ½ cup of the cream and process until just blended. Push the mixture through a sieve, cover and refrigerate for 2 hours.

3 Using a wooden spoon, mix in the remaining ½ cup of cream.

Poached Prawns in Pernod (top); Fish Mousseline with Shallot Cream Sauce

4 Bring a saucepan of water to the boil, reduce heat and simmer. Shape mousseline mixture into a ball with a dessert spoon and slide shaped mixture into simmering water; poach for 1 minute.

5 Remove mousseline with slotted spoon and place on absorbent paper.

6 In a frying pan, add the extra cream and wine and bring to the boil over medium heat. Reduce heat and simmer 5 minutes or until sauce thickens slightly. Mix in spring onions and serve over mousseline.

Serves 4

Marinated Red Capsicum (Pepper)

4 large red capsicum (pepper)

2 tblspn olive oil

2 small cloves garlic, very thinly sliced

1 Grill capsicum until blackened, place in a paper bag, seal well, leave for 10 minutes. Remove from bag, peel off skin and remove seeds and any thick ribs.

2 Cut into long strips. Place in a bowl. Add olive oil and garlic. Season to taste with salt and freshly ground black pepper.

3 Cover, stand at room temperature for 1 hour. Serve with fresh Italian bread slices or crackers.

Serves 4

Gruyere Quiche

½ x 375g (¾lb) packet prepared shortcrust pastry

5 large eggs

2 cups cream

125g (4oz) Gruyere cheese, grated

Cherry Tomatoes with Parmesan and Rosemary (top); Grilled Eggplant Aubergine) with Mozzarella Cheese

1 Roll pastry to fit a 23cm (9in) quiche dish. Line pastry with foil, sprinkle with dried beans. Bake in moderately hot oven 8 minutes. Remove foil and beans, bake a further 10 minutes or until golden.

2 In a bowl combine 2 whole eggs with 3 yolks; reserve remaining egg whites for another use, eg. meringues (see the index). Add cream, season to taste with salt and freshly ground white pepper, add Gruyere.

3 Pour egg mixture into the tart shell, bake in the middle of a 160°C (325°F) oven for 45 minutes, or until set and the top is golden. Stand at room temperature for at least 20 minutes, serve warm.

Serves 8

Cherry Tomatoes with Parmesan and Rosemary

1 punnet cherry tomatoes, halved and seeded

black pepper

¼ cup grated Parmesan cheese

1 tblspn cream

pinch nutmeg

1 tablespoon fresh rosemary, finely chopped

1 Sprinkle the inside of tomatoes with black pepper.

2 In a small bowl, combine cheese, cream, nutmeg and rosemary, mix well.

3 Spoon mixture into the tomatoes and grill for 1 minute. Serve immediately.

Serves 4

Grilled Eggplant (Aubergine) with Mozzarella Cheese

1 medium eggplant (aubergine), cut into 1cm (½in) slices

3 tblspn olive oil

1 garlic clove, crushed

¼ tspn pepper

8 thin slices mozzarella

2 pimentos, sliced into strips

1 Lightly brush eggplant slices with combined oil, garlic and pepper. Grill until lightly browned, approximately 3 minutes each side.

2 Top each slice with mozzarella cheese and decorate with pimento strips.

3 Return to the grill and cook until cheese has melted. Serve immediately and garnish with fresh basil if desired.

Makes 8

Crudite with Eggplant and Olive Puree

1 large eggplant (aubergine)

2 cloves garlic, peeled

½ cup olives, pitted

about 1 tblspn olive oil

a mixture of raw vegetables, eg. carrot sticks, cauliflowerets, zucchini (courgette) sticks, red and green capsicum (pepper) sticks

1 Bake eggplant in a hot oven until soft, about 40 minutes. Cut in half lengthwise and allow to cool.

2 Plunge garlic into a small amount of boiling water, cook 15 minutes. Drain, peel.

3 Remove eggplant pulp from skins, combine in a processor with garlic and olives. Add 2 teaspoons oil. Add salt and freshly ground black pepper to taste. Puree until smooth. Add more oil if necessary.

4 Transfer to a serving dish. Serve with raw vegetables for dipping.

Makes about 2 cups

SIDE SALADS

Goodbye boring salads! We've used a variety of tastes and textures in these recipes to create truly delicious salads — and they not only taste good, they're good for you too.

Avocado, Grapefruit and Spanish Onion Salad

1 large grapefruit, peeled, all pith removed, segmented

2 avocados, peeled, seeded, cubed

2 tblspn lemon juice

¼ cup mayonnaise

cos lettuce leaves, cleaned

1 small Spanish onion, thinly sliced

1 Cut grapefruit segments into bite-size pieces. Sprinkle avocado cubes with 1 tablespoon lemon juice.

2 Combine remaining tablespoon of lemon juice with mayonnaise, whisk until well mixed. Season to taste with salt, freshly ground pepper and more lemon juice if desired.

3 Arrange lettuce leaves on 4 plates. Toss avocado with grapefruit, divide among plates. Top with onion slices. Drizzle with mayonnaise dressing. Serve immediately.

Serves 4

Mushroom Salad

500g (1lb) mushrooms

½ cup olive oil

2 tblspn red wine vinegar

¼ cup chopped parsley

1 tblspn freshly squeezed lemon juice

1 Trim mushrooms, wipe with a damp towel, slice thinly. Place in a salad bowl.

2 In a screwtop jar combine oil, vinegar, parsley and lemon juice. Season to taste with salt and freshly ground black pepper. Shake until well combined.

3 Pour over mushrooms in bowl, toss well to coat. Stand at least 30 minutes at room temperature before serving.

Serves 4

Avocado, Feta and Bacon Salad

a selection of lettuce leaves, washed and dried

2 ripe avocados

juice of lemon

3 tblspn olive oil

250g (½lb) streaky bacon, cut diagonally into strips, cook until crisp

250g (½lb) Feta cheese, cut into small cubes

1 Arrange lettuce on a platter or in a dish, halve, peel and remove stones from avocado. Slice and toss in lemon juice, arrange on lettuce.

2 Combine olive oil and remaining lemon juice in a pan, heat until hot; then add bacon.

3 Arrange Feta over top of salad, quickly pour hot bacon dressing over salad and serve immediately.

Serves 6

Avocado, Feta and Bacon Salad

Choko (Chayote), Hearts of Palm and Zucchini (Courgette) Salad

1 cup well-seasoned garlicky vinaigrette

½ cup chopped parsley

2 chokos (chayote), peeled, seeded, cut into julienne sticks

3 canned hearts of palm, drained, cut into julienne sticks

2 yellow zucchini (courgette), unpeeled, cut into julienne sticks

salad greens

1 Combine vinaigrette with parsley, place in a large bowl.

2 Plunge choko into lightly salted boiling water, allow water to return to the boil, boil 5 minutes. Drain, cool.

3 Combine choko in bowl with dressing and hearts of palm and zucchini. Stand at room temperature about 2 hours.

4 Arrange salad greens on plates, top with marinated vegetables, add any remaining dressing. Serve at room temperature.

Serves 6

Spicy Cucumber and Fruit Salad

4 cucumbers, peeled

½ rockmelon, seeds removed

1 punnet of strawberries

2 tblspn lime juice

1 tblspn finely chopped fresh coriander

1 Using a melon-baller scoop cucumber and rockmelon into balls, place in bowl.

2 Add strawberries, lime juice and coriander.

Serves 4

Spicy Cucumber and Fruit Salad (left, top) and Apple and Watercress Salad with Blue Cheese; Bean Salad with Artichokes (above)

Apple and Watercress Salad with Blue Cheese

2 green apples

1 bunch watercress

½ Spanish onion, sliced

¼ cup chopped chives

155g (5oz) blue vein cheese, crumbled

4 tblspn French dressing

1 Core apples and chop into wedges.

2 Wash cress, dry in a tea-towel and discard coarse stems. Chop cress and place in a large bowl with apples, add onion and chives.

3 Crumble cheese over top of salad and pour over dressing.

Serves 4

Bean Salad with Artichokes

2 cups green beans

1 red capsicum (pepper)

1 cup butter beans, drained and washed

1 cup artichoke hearts, cut in halves

2 tblspn olive oil

4 tblspn vinegar

1 Cut tops and tails off beans. Cook beans in 2cm (¾in) of boiling water for 2 minutes, drain, run cold water over beans to cool.

2 Cut capsicum into very fine strips and place in a dish of ice water for 20 minutes, or until curled.

3 Toss together beans, butter beans, artichokes and capsicum, pour over combined olive oil and vinegar.

Serves 4

Autumn Salad

1 thick slice ham, about 125g (4oz)

1 red capsicum (pepper)

750g (1½lb) broccoli

2 Granny Smith apples

¼ cup freshly squeezed lemon juice

½ cup walnut oil

1 Cut ham into 1cm (½in) cubes. Cut capsicum in half, remove seeds and membranes, cut into thin strips.

2 Add ham, capsicum and broccoli to a pot of very lightly salted boiling water. Cook 5 minutes over medium heat. Drain, refresh under cold running water. Drain, cool.

3 Divide broccoli into flowerets, cut stems into small dice.

4 Core and coarsely dice apples, don't peel. Toss in a salad bowl with lemon juice. Add ham, capsicum and broccoli. Pour over walnut oil, toss gently. Season to taste with salt and freshly ground pepper, toss again. Serve immediately.

Serves 6

Mixed Green Salad with Anchovy Dressing

4 cups mixed salad greens, eg. watercress and cos lettuce

¼ cup olive oil

1 tblspn red wine vinegar

6 flat anchovy fillets, cut into ¼cm (1/8in) dice

4 spring onions (scallions), white part only, thinly sliced

1 Tear lettuce into bite-size pieces. Place in a salad bowl.

2 In a small bowl combine oil, vinegar, anchovies and spring onions. Whisk until well combined. Season to taste with salt and freshly ground pepper.

3 Pour over salad greens, toss to mix evenly.

Serves 4

Beet and Carrot Salad

Beet and Carrot Salad

6 medium beets

8 medium carrots

4 hard-boiled eggs

4 tblspn vinegar

2 tblspn lemon juice

1 Peel beets and boil whole until tender, cool to room temperature. Slice into julienne strips.

2 Peel carrots and slice as beets.

3 Slice boiled eggs and add to carrot and beet mixture.

4 Mix vinegar and lemon juice together, season to taste, add to salad, toss well.

Serves 4

Cucumber Salad Japanese Style

2 tspn sesame seeds

2 cucumbers, peeled, seeds removed, thinly sliced

1 tblspn rice vinegar

½ tspn light brown sugar

¼ tspn salt

1/8 tspn Tabasco sauce

1 Add sesame seeds to a dry frying pan. Shake pan over moderate heat until seeds start to pop. Remove from pan, cool.

2 Place cucumber slices in a colander, place a plate on top, weighed down with a heavy object, eg. a large can. Leave to drain for at least 30 minutes.

Spinach Grapefruit Salad

3 Place cucumbers in a bowl, toss with combined vinegar, sugar and salt. Sprinkle with Tabasco and sesame seeds. Serve immediately.

Serves 6

Tomato Salad Napolitano

1kg (2lb) ripe tomatoes, cut into 8 wedges each

1 Spanish onion, thinly sliced

1½ cups coarsely grated Pecorino cheese

1 cup vinaigrette

1 tblspn chopped fresh basil

2 tspn chopped fresh oregano

1 In a large bowl combine tomatoes with onion and cheese. Mix well.

2 In a small bowl combine vinaigrette with basil and oregano. Pour over tomatoes, toss well. Serve at room temperature.

Serves 6

Spinach Grapefruit Salad

1 bunch fresh spinach, stemmed and washed

1 large grapefruit, segmented

½ Spanish onion, peeled, chopped into small cubes

1 cup red cabbage, sliced finely

¼ cup French dressing

3 tblspn orange juice, freshly squeezed

1 Tear spinach into bite-size pieces and place in salad bowl.

2 Add grapefruit, onion and cabbage, toss well.

3 Mix dressing and orange juice together, pour over salad just before serving. Garnish with thin strips of orange rind if desired.

Serves 4

Crisp Celery Salad

1 bunch celery

5 tblspn olive oil

2 tblspn white wine vinegar

1½ tspn Dijon mustard

1 Trim celery stalks, cut into julienne sticks about ¼ cm (1/8in) thick. Plunge sticks into lightly salted boiling water, allow water to return to the boil, drain immediately. Refresh in a large bowl of iced water. Drain thoroughly.

2 In a large bowl toss celery with olive oil. Stand 1 hour at room temperature.

3 In a small bowl whisk vinegar with mustard. Add salt and freshly ground pepper to taste. Add to celery, toss well.

Serves 8

Rockmelon (Cantaloupe), Cucumber and Pear Salad

1½ cup rockmelon (cantaloupe), cubed

1½ cup cucumber, peeled, seeds removed, cubed

1½ cup pears, peeled, cored, cubed

¼ cup white wine vinegar

⅓ cup olive oil

curly endive

1 Combine melon, cucumber and pear in a bowl. Add white wine vinegar, toss well to coat.

2 Add salt and freshly ground pepper to taste. Add oil, toss thoroughly to coat every piece.

3 Arrange salad on a bed of curly endive. Serve at room temperature.

Serves 6

Witlof (Chicory, Belgian Endive) and Avocado Salad

½ cup vinaigrette

1 tspn freshly chopped fresh tarragon, or ¼ tspn dried

2 avocados

1 tblspn freshly squeezed lemon juice

3 heads witlof (US chicory, US Belgian endive)

watercress

1 Combine vinaigrette with tarragon. Whisk vigorously to combine, set aside for at least 15 minutes.

2 Peel and seed avocados, cut lengthwise into thin slices. Sprinkle with lemon juice.

3 Separate witlof leaves, cut large leaves in half. Arrange witlof and avocados on a platter with watercress.

4 Pour over vinaigrette, season to taste with salt and freshly ground black pepper. Serve immediately.

Serves 6

Snow Pea Salad

500g (1lb) snow peas, trimmed

2 tblspn lemon juice

2 tspn light soy sauce

⅓ cup walnut oil

3 spring onions (scallions), sliced diagonally

2 tspn grated fresh ginger

1 Plunge snow peas into lightly salted boiling water, allow water to return to the boil. Cook about 30 seconds.

2 Drain, rinse under cold running water to preserve colour, drain, pat dry with paper towels. Place in a serving dish.

3 Combine lemon juice and soy sauce in a screwtop jar. Add walnut oil. Shake until well combined. Add spring onion and ginger, shake again.

4 Pour dressing over the snow peas, toss until well coated.

Serves 4

Salad of Capsicum (Pepper) and Mushrooms with Garlic Dressing

2 red capsicum (pepper)

2 green capsicum (pepper)

250g (½lb) button mushrooms, sliced

2 cloves garlic, crushed

2 tblspn red wine vinegar

2 tspn olive oil

1 Steam capsicum for 5 minutes, cut into julienne strips.

2 Mix capsicum strips and mushrooms.

3 In a dish, combine garlic, vinegar and oil, pour over salad, toss well.

Serves 4

Crunchy Potato Salad (top); Salad of Capsicum (Pepper) and Mushrooms with Garlic Dressing

Crunchy Potato Salad

5 large potatoes, peeled, cut into cubes

1 cup cocktail onions, drained

8 hard-boiled eggs

¼ cup capers, drained

¾ cup olive oil

½ cup toasted pinenuts

1 Boil potatoes until tender, cool to room temperature. Place in a large salad bowl.

2 Add remaining ingredients and toss gently. Season with salt and pepper to taste.

Serves 4

Fennel Salad with Parmesan Cheese

1 large fennel bulb with stalk and fronds

¼ cup lemon juice

⅓ cup olive oil

1 tspn freshly ground pepper

¼ cup julienned orange peel

60g (2oz) piece Parmesan cheese

1 Cut fronds from the top of fennel bulbs, reserve about half a cup. Discard stalks. Cut bulb into paper-thin slices. Place in a salad bowl.

2 In a small bowl combine lemon juice with olive oil, whisk until amalgamated. Add half a teaspoon of pepper.

3 Add dressing to fennel slices in salad bowl, toss with julienned orange peel and fennel fronds. Divide mixture evenly among 4 plates.

4 With a cheese slicer cut paper-thin slices of Parmesan, arrange over fennel. Sprinkle with remaining black pepper. Serve at room temperature.

Serves 4

MAKE MORE OF MEAT

It's important to include meat in a well-balanced diet and with these recipes you'll be able to prepare mouthwatering meals in no time at all.

Saddle of Lamb with Mustard Sauce

2 cloves garlic crushed

2 tblspn Dijon mustard

2 tblspn grain mustard

2 tblspn tarragon vinegar

1 kg (2lb) saddle of lamb

30g (1oz) fine breadcrumbs

1 Trim and bone saddle. Brush the combined garlic, Dijon mustard, grain mustard and vinegar over lamb. Tie lamb with string to secure and bake in moderate oven 20 minutes.

2 Remove from oven and sprinkle the lamb with breadcrumbs; pressing them into the meat lightly.

3 Return to oven and cook a further 15 minutes. Serve with baked vegetables if desired.

Serves 4

Lamb Fillets in Rosemary Sauce

3 tblspn chopped fresh rosemary or 1 tblspn dried

2 cups chicken stock

4 lamb fillets, about 220g (7oz) each

about 2 tblspn olive oil

5 tblspn butter

1 If using fresh rosemary, add 2 tablespoons to chicken stock, if using dried, use 1 tablespoon. Bring to a boil, reduce over medium heat to ½ cup. Strain.

2 Cut lamb fillets into 0.5cm (¼ in) thick slices. Season to taste with salt and freshly ground black pepper.

3 Heat 1 tablespoon oil in a frying pan, add lamb in batches, without crowding the pan, brown very quickly on both sides. Remove from pan, keep warm. Add more oil if necessary.

4 Pour any remaining oil from pan, add stock, heat, scrape up any brown bits from bottom of pan. If using fresh rosemary, add remaining tablespoon.

5 Remove from heat, whisk in butter little by little, until sauce thickens. Correct seasoning.

6 Divide lamb among 4 heated plates, pour sauce around lamb, serve hot.

Serves 4

Saddle of Lamb with Mustard Marinade

Veal Chops with Tarragon Sauce

4 veal loin chops, 2.5cm (1in) thick

1 tblspn dried tarragon, crumbled

¼ cup butter

½ cup dry red wine

1 Dry veal chops thoroughly on paper towels, season to taste with salt and freshly ground black pepper. Sprinkle with tarragon, press well into the meat.

2 Melt butter in a frying pan over moderately high heat. When foamy add chops. Brown on both sides, turning several times, about 8 minutes. Remove from pan, keep warm.

3 Add wine, cook, scraping up any brown bits from the bottom of the pan, reduce to ⅓ cup, about 4 minutes. Serve chops on heated plates, pour over sauce.

Serves 4

Saltimbocca

8 slices veal scallops, flattened

8 slices prosciutto, roughly same size as scallops

8 fresh sage leaves

¼ cup olive oil

1 tblspn butter

1 cup dry white wine

1 Place 1 sage leaf on top of each slice of veal, top with prosciutto. Fasten with a toothpick, leave meat flat.

2 Combine butter and oil in a frying pan. Fry veal over medium high heat until brown on both sides. Season to taste with salt, add wine. Simmer 10 minutes.

3 Remove veal slices to a heated platter, keep warm.

4 Bring juices to a boil, reduce to half their volume. Pour juices over veal and serve hot.

Serves 4

Roast Veal Fillet with Peppercorn Sauce

4 tblspn butter

1kg (2lb) veal fillet

1½ cups cream

1 cup chicken stock

¼ cup dry white wine

1 tblspn green peppercorns

1 Melt butter in a heavy-based saucepan over high heat. Add the veal, turning regularly, until cooked on outside and golden brown.

2 Transfer fillet to a baking dish, cook in moderate oven 35-40 minutes or until just cooked inside.

3 Add cream, stock, wine and peppercorns to frying pan, cook over high heat until reduced by half. Slice veal, pour over sauce.

Serves 4

Parmesan Coated Deep-fried Lamb Cutlets

8 lamb cutlets, 125g (4oz) each

2 eggs, beaten

1 cup dry breadcrumbs

¼ cup freshly grated Parmesan cheese

1 tblspn chopped fresh basil

1 tblspn crushed garlic

1 Season lamb with salt and freshly ground black pepper. Dust cutlets with flour, shake off excess.

2 Place beaten eggs in a deep plate. Combine breadcrumbs, cheese, basil and garlic in another plate.

3 Dip cutlets into eggs first, then breadcrumb mixture, pressing down to coat thoroughly.

4 Deep-fry cutlets in oil, about 10 minutes for medium-rare, turning occasionally. Drain on paper towels. Serve on heated plates.

Serves 4

Roast Veal Fillet with Peppercorn Sauce (top); Veal with Mozzarella

Veal with Mozzarella

4 tblspn butter

4 veal fillets

¼ cup wine

2 cups canned peeled tomatoes

1 tspn finely chopped basil

2 cups grated mozzarella

1 Heat butter in a large frying pan, add veal fillets and cook over medium heat for 1 minute each side. Remove veal and keep warm in oven.

2 Add wine to frying pan and reduce by half. Add tomatoes and basil and cook over medium heat for 5 minutes.

3 Place veal fillets in baking dish, top with tomato sauce and sprinkle with mozzarella cheese. Bake in a moderately hot oven for 10 minutes or just until cheese has melted.

Serves 4

Lamb Chops with Minted Whisky Sauce

8 lamb loin chops, 125g (4oz)

⅓ cup butter

SAUCE:

1 cup mint leaves

½ cup sugar

¼ cup white wine vinegar

2 tblspn Scotch whisky

1 To make sauce: Combine all ingredients in a processor. Blend until smooth. Remove to a bowl, cover, chill.

2 Dry chops well on paper towels. Season to taste with salt and freshly ground black pepper.

3 Fry in butter, grill or barbecue until done to your liking, about 3 minutes each side for rare.

4 Serve hot, spoon over sauce.

Serves 4

Sirloin Patties with Goats Cheese and Tomato

Sirloin Patties with Goats Cheese and Tomato

2 tblspn butter

500g (1lb) minced sirloin, shaped into 4 patties 1cm (½in) thick

100g (3½oz) goats cheese, grated

1 tomato, cut into slices, each slice cut into quarters

1 tblspn chopped chives

curly endive lettuce

1 Melt butter in a large frying pan over medium heat. Add the patties and cook for 3 minutes each side.

2 Remove patties from pans and top with sliced tomato, and cheese.

3 Place patties under a grill, cook until cheese melts, serve immediately. Decorate with chopped chives and endive.

Serves 4

Veal with Mushroom and Parmesan Cream Sauce

60g (2oz) dried porcini mushrooms*

6 slices veal scallops, about 500g (1lb)

300ml (½ pint) cream

155g (5oz) freshly grated Parmesan cheese

2 eggs, beaten

60g (2oz) unsalted butter

* Porcini mushrooms are available at Italian grocery stores.

1 Soak mushrooms in warm water for 30 minutes, drain, chop. Beat veal slices with a mallet to flatten.

2 Combine mushrooms, cream and 90g (3oz) of the Parmesan in a saucepan. Cook over moderate heat for 15 minutes, season to taste with salt and freshly ground black pepper. Keep warm.

3 In a deep plate combine beaten eggs with remaining Parmesan, season to taste with salt. Dip scallops into the mixture, turn to coat well.

4 Heat butter in a frying pan, when foamy add scallops, cook until golden brown on both sides.

5 Place meat on heated plates, pour over cream sauce. Serve immediately.

Serves 6

Pork Chops with Neapolitan Sauce

4 pork loin chops

½ cup olive oil

2 cloves garlic, chopped

2 cups chopped tomatoes, peeled, seeded

1 cup sliced button mushrooms

3 green capsicum (peppers)

1 Remove fat from chops, leave bones on, flatten to 0.5cm (¼in) thickness. Season to taste with salt and freshly ground black pepper, dust with flour.

Glazed Beef Ribs with Redcurrant Sauce

2 Heat 5 tablespoons oil in a frying pan, add garlic, saute until brown. Add chops, cook over medium heat until both sides are brown. Remove chops, keep warm.

3 Add tomatoes, season with a little salt and freshly ground pepper. Simmer 5 minutes. Add mushrooms, simmer a further 5 minutes. Return pork chops to pan, cook 15 minutes over moderate heat. If sauce thickens too much, add some water.

4 Grill capsicum until skin blisters and blackens. Place in a paper bag, seal, leave to steam 10 minutes. Rub skin off. Remove seeds and inner membranes, cut into large strips.

5 Place remaining oil in a frying pan, saute capsicum until tender. Season with salt, keep hot.

6 Place pork chops on a heated serving platter, cover with hot capsicum and tomato sauce.

Serves 4

Glazed Beef Ribs with Redcurrant Sauce

4 beef ribs, trimmed

2 tblspn redcurrant jelly

2 tblspn honey

1 tblspn plum conserve

¼ cup lemon juice

2 tblspn rosemary

1 Cut each rib into 3 pieces. In a large frying pan, add redcurrant jelly, honey, plum conserve and lemon juice.

2 Bring mixture to the boil, add rib pieces and cook in redcurrant sauce until dark brown, stirring all the time, approximately 10 minutes.

3 Add rosemary, cook further 1 minute. Serve immediately.

Serves 4

Steak Tartare

Ask your butcher to mince fillet steak for you, or do it yourself in a food processor.

500g (1lb) fillet steak, minced

1 onion, finely chopped

1 tblspn capers, finely chopped

6 anchovy fillets, finely chopped

¼ tspn Tabasco sauce, or more to taste

2 tblspn olive oil*

* Some people like Steak Tartare served with a raw egg yolk, placed in an indentation on top of the meat. If serving Steak Tartare in this fashion, omit olive oil in the mixture.

1 In a bowl combine all ingredients. Season to taste with salt and freshly ground black pepper.

2 Divide mixture into four balls, flatten into patties. Serve with warm toast triangles.

Serves 4

Leg of Lamb with Plum Sauce

1.5kg (3lb) leg of lamb

1 cup red wine

1 onion, chopped

16 plums, halved, stoned

¼ tspn allspice

1 tblspn red wine vinegar

1 Season lamb with salt and freshly ground black pepper. Baste with wine, roast in a moderate oven until done to your liking. Halfway through cooking time add onion and plums to roasting pan. Baste from time to time.

2 When meat is cooked, remove to a hot dish, stand in a warm place at least 15 minutes before carving.

3 Sieve contents of roasting pan, reserve liquid, force solids through sieve into a saucepan. Skim fat from liquid, add juices to saucepan. Boil to reduce if necessary. Add allspice and vinegar. Pour into a sauceboat.

4 Carve meat, arrange on heated serving platter. Serve warm with plum sauce.

Serves 6

Chilli Beef Shanks

16 dried red chillies*

1 tspn cumin seed

400g (13oz) can tomatoes, drained

3 cloves garlic, crushed

1.5kg (3lb) beef shank, cut into 3.5cm (1½in) slices

⅓ cup chopped fresh coriander

* Use more if you like it really hot

1 Combine chillies and cumin seed in a processor, add 2½ cups boiling water. Stand 30 minutes to soften chillies. Puree, pour into a baking dish large enough to hold shanks in one layer.

2 In the processor combine tomatoes with garlic and 1½ teaspoons salt. Puree, add to baking dish. Mix well.

3 Add shanks, turn to coat meat on all sides. Cover dish securely with foil.

4 Bake for 3 hours in a 160°C (325°F) oven, or until meat is tender, turning once during cooking. Remove foil, bake a further 30 minutes. If sauce seems too thin, pour into a saucepan and cook over high heat to reduce. Serve hot, sprinkled with coriander.

Serves 6

Minted Tandoori Lamb

1 cup plain yoghurt

1 tblspn ground cumin

1 tblspn ground coriander

2 tblspn mild curry powder

4 lamb chump chops, each chop cut into three pieces

1 tblspn fresh mint, chopped

1 In a small bowl, combine yoghurt, cumin, curry powder and coriander, mix well.

2 Toss pieces of lamb in yoghurt mixture, coat evenly. Place lamb on a rack which is standing inside a baking dish.

3 Bake in a moderate oven for 45 minutes, turning lamb every 15 minutes.

4 Sprinkle mint over lamb and serve immediately.

Serves 2

Minted Tandoori Lamb

Ham Steaks with Marsala Sauce

6 ham steaks, 1cm (½in) thick, fat removed
5 tblspn unsalted butter
½ cup chicken stock
½ cup Marsala
½ tspn grated lemon rind
¼ cup chopped parsley

1 Saute ham steaks over moderate heat in a frying pan in 2 tablespoons butter until lightly browned, about 3 minutes each side. Work in batches. Keep warm. Pour off fat in frying pan.

2 Add stock, Marsala and lemon rind to the frying pan, bring to a boil, scrape up any brown bits from the bottom of the pan. Reduce liquid to ½ cup, about 5 minutes.

3 Off the heat, whisk in remaining butter, little by little. Stir in parsley.

4 Return ham and accumulated juices to the pan, heat through if necessary, turning once to coat. Serve ham steaks on a heated platter, serve sauce separately in a heated sauceboat.

Serves 6

Minced Beefsteak with Smoked Ham

750g (1½lb) minced topside
125g (4oz) smoked ham, chopped
2 egg yolks
2 tblspn butter

1 Combine mince and ham in a bowl. Add egg yolks, season to taste with salt and freshly ground black pepper.

2 Shape into 4 equal balls, flatten with your hand. Dust lightly with flour, shaking off excess.

3 Melt butter in frying pan over high heat until foam subsides. Add meat and fry on both sides until done to your liking. Serve hot.

Serves 4

Honey Beef Fillet with Stuffed Tomatoes

1kg (2lb) eye fillet of beef

2 tblspn butter, 3 tblspn butter extra

2 tblspn honey

8 small tomatoes

1 cup dried breadcrumbs

¼ cup grated mozzarella cheese

1 Trim away any excess fat from beef.

2 Melt 2 tablespoons butter with honey in a large frying pan. Add beef and cook over a high heat until outside is golden brown, approximately 4 minutes.

3 Transfer fillet to a medium baking dish and cook in moderate oven 35-40 minutes, or until cooked through.

4 Cut tops off tomatoes and scoop out centres, discard. Melt 3 extra tablespoons butter and mix into combined breadcrumbs and cheese.

5 Spoon breadcrumb mixture back into tomatoes and grill for 1 minute, or until tops are golden. Serve beef in 1cm (½in) thick slices with tomatoes. Garnish with fresh herbs if desired.

Serves 4

Beef Scallops with Capers

8 thin slices fillet steak, about 90g (30oz) each

5 tblspn butter

2 tblspn oil

¼ cup capers

1 tblspn chopped continental parsley

3 tblspn red wine vinegar

1 Beat beef slices with a mallet to 1cm (½in) thickness. Season to taste with salt and freshly ground black pepper. Dust with flour, shake to rid of excess.

2 Add butter and oil to a frying pan, heat until butter foam subsides. Add beef slices, brown on both sides.

3 Add capers and parsley with 2 tablespoons water. Cook a further 5 minutes, turning beef occasionally.

4 In a small saucepan reduce vinegar to 1 tablespoon over high heat, pour over beef, mix well. Place slices on a heated platter, pour over pan juices. Serve hot.

Serves 4

Grilled Lamb Noisettes with Balsamic Vinegar Sauce

4 lamb noisettes, about 185g (6oz)

SAUCE:

½ cup dry white wine

2 rosemary sprigs

1½ tspn balsamic vinegar

¼ tspn cracked black pepper

2 cups beef stock

1 To make the sauce: Combine wine, rosemary, vinegar and pepper in a heavy saucepan. Boil over high heat until reduced to 2 tablespoons, about 5 minutes.

2 Add stock, boil a further 20 minutes, or until reduced to 5 tablespoons.

3 Grill or barbecue noisettes until done to your liking, about 5 minutes both sides for rare lamb.

4 Reheat sauce, strain. Season to taste with salt and freshly ground black pepper. Arrange noisettes on heated plates. Serve hot napped with sauce.

Serves 4

Jamaican Veal Stew

750g (1½lb) veal, cut into 2.5cm (1in) cubes

2 tblspn peanut oil

1 large onion, chopped

1 cup chicken stock

1 cup canned unsweetened pineapple pieces, reserve ¼ cup juice

½ cup sliced mushrooms

Honey Beef Fillet with Stuffed Tomatoes

1 Dry pieces of veal well on paper towels, season to taste with salt and freshly ground black pepper. Dust with flour.

2 Heat peanut oil in a frying pan, add veal cubes, brown on all sides. Remove from pan, set aside.

3 Add onion to frying pan, saute until golden, about 5 minutes. Add stock, return veal to pan, combine well. Cover, simmer until veal is tender, about 30 minutes.

4 Add pineapple, juice and mushrooms, simmer until heated through, about 10 minutes. Check seasoning. Serve on heated plates.

Serves 4

Lamb Fillets with Blueberries

4 lamb fillets, 100g (3½oz) each

3 tblspn butter

1 garlic clove, crushed

2 cups canned blueberries and juice

½ cup brown sugar

¼ cup lemon juice

1 Heat the butter, with the crushed garlic, in a medium frying pan. Add fillets and cook for 3-4 minutes, turning frequently. Remove fillets from pan and keep warm in oven.

2 Add blueberries and blueberry juice, sugar and lemon juice to pan. Slowly bring to the boil, reduce heat and simmer for 20 minutes, or until sauce has thickened slightly.

3 Cut fillet into diagonal slices, arrange in a fan on serving plate, and pour over sauce. Serve with vegetables if desired.

Serves 4

Lamb Fillet with Blueberries

Skewered Pork and Sausages with Prosciutto

Skewered Pork and Sausages with Prosciutto

¼ loaf of day-old bread, crusts removed, cut into 2cm (¾in) cubes

4 hot Italian sausages

250g (½lb) pork fillet

2 capsicum (pepper), 1 red, 1 green, cut into 2cm (¾in) cubes

1 cup tinned baby corn, cut into 2cm (¾in) lengths

90g (3oz) thinly sliced prosciutto, cut into strips 2cm (¾in) wide

1 Soak 8 wooden skewers in warm water for 1 hour.

2 Bring a large saucepan of water to the boil, add sausages, cook for 8 minutes.

3 Remove sausages and cut into 2cm (¾in) lengths. Cut pork fillet into 2cm (¾in) cubes.

4 Thread pieces of corn, pork, capsicum and sausage onto skewers, along with a cube of bread on the top.

5 Grill kebabs for 2 minutes each side or until pork is just cooked.

6 Remove from heat and wrap a strip of prosciutto around the pork pieces. Return to heat and grill a further 1 minute each side. Serve immediately.

Serves 4

Pork Fillets with Mustard Sauce

2 pork fillets, each 500g (1lb)

⅓ cup whole grain mustard

2 tblspn melted lard

1 cup dry vermouth

2 tblspn plain flour

2 tblspn unsalted butter, softened

1 Cut fillets diagonally into 8 slices, arrange in a greased baking dish just large enough to hold slices in 1 layer. Add salt and freshly ground black pepper to taste, spread mustard on top.

2 Drizzle with lard, pour vermouth into the dish, cover securely with foil. Bake in a 180°C (350°F) oven for 30 minutes, basting with cooking juices twice. Divide pork between 4 heated plates, keep warm. Pour juices into a saucepan.

3 In a small bowl combine flour and softened butter, mix well. Whisk little by little into the juices in the saucepan, cooking over moderately high heat, stirring constantly, until sauce thickens.

4 Spoon sauce over pork slices, serve immediately.

Serves 4

Pork Scallops with Tangy Raisin Sauce

Pork Medallions with Tangy Ginger Sauce

8 pork medallions, 1cm (½in) thick

½ cup unsalted butter

2 tblspn freshly grated ginger

2 tblspn red wine vinegar

⅔ cup chicken stock

¼ cup finely chopped parsley

1 Dry slices of pork thoroughly on paper towels, dust with flour.

2 Melt 2 tablespoons butter in a frying pan until foaming. Saute half the pork slices until one side is brown, about 4 minutes. Brown other side, a further 4 minutes. Remove, keep warm on a serving platter. Brown remaining pork, remove, keep warm.

3 Pour off excess fat in frying pan. Add ginger and vinegar, bring to a boil, scrape up any brown bits from the bottom of the pan. Boil about 3 minutes.

4 Add chicken stock, reduce liquid to ⅓ cup over high heat.

5 Off the heat whisk in remaining butter little by little. Add any accumulated meat juices from platter. Stir in 2 tablespoons parsley. Season to taste with salt and freshly ground pepper. Pour over pork on platter, sprinkle with remaining parsley.

Serves 4

Pork Scallops with Tangy Raisin Sauce

½ cup raisins

1 cup chicken stock

500g (1lb) pork tenderloin

6 tblspn butter

¾ cup plain flour

⅓ cup cherry vinegar

1 Place raisins in a medium bowl, bring stock to the boil and pour over raisins, stand for 1 hour.

2 Cut 1cm thick (½in) slices from tenderloin, pound a little with a meat pounder. Dredge slices in flour, shaking off excess.

3 Melt 3 tablespoons of the butter in a large frying pan, add pork scallops and cook for 3 minutes each side. Remove pork and keep warm in a low oven.

4 Add the vinegar to the pan, scraping up any browned bits from the bottom of the pan, bring to the boil and simmer until vinegar has thickened.

5 Add raisins and stock and bring to the boil, reduce heat and simmer 5 minutes.

6 Reduce heat to low and whisk in remaining 3 tablespoons of butter. Serve over pork scallops with vegetables if desired.

Serves 3-4

Pork Chops with Mustard Cheese Crust

½ cup finely grated Parmesan

3 tblspn mango chutney, plus ⅓ cup extra

1 tblspn Dijon mustard

1 tblspn grain mustard

2 x 2½cm thick loin pork chops

¾ cup wholemeal dried breadcrumbs

1 In a small bowl, combine Parmesan cheese with 3 tablespoons of mango chutney, Dijon mustard and grain mustard, mix well.

2 Trim excess fat from chops, brush generously with the mango mustard mixture and dredge the chops in breadcrumbs.

3 Place chops on a rack, standing within a baking tray. Bake in moderate oven for 25-30 minutes, turning chops occasionally during baking.

4 Serve chops with vegetables and extra chutney if desired.

Serves 2

Beef Stroganoff

500g (1lb) fillet of beef, all visible fat and sinew removed

2 tblspn butter

1 onion, sliced

155g (5oz) button mushrooms, wiped clean, sliced

2 tspn tomato paste

½ cup sour cream

1 Cut beef into thin strips. Season to taste with salt and freshly ground black pepper. Dust with a little flour.

2 Melt 1 tablespoon butter in a frying pan, add onion, saute over gentle heat until golden, about 10 minutes. Add mushrooms, saute about 4 minutes. Remove onions and mushrooms to a plate.

3 Add remaining tablespoon of butter to the frying pan. When very hot add beef and stir-fry over a brisk heat until brown all over, about 3 minutes.

4 Return onions and mushrooms to the pan, heat through. Add tomato paste and sour cream, correct seasoning, cook gently until heated through. Serve hot.

Serves 4

Pork and Cabbage Casserole

1 small cabbage, finely sliced

1 cup cream

4 pork loin chops, fat removed

¼ cup butter

½ cup white wine

⅓ cup freshly grated Parmesan cheese

1 Plunge cabbage into lightly salted boiling water. Boil 6 minutes. Drain, return to saucepan, add salt and freshly ground pepper to taste, add cream, simmer, covered for 30 minutes. Keep warm.

2 Saute pork chops in a frying pan in 2 tablespoons butter until browned on both sides and cooked through, about 30 minutes, turning from time to time. Remove, season to taste with salt and freshly ground black pepper.

3 Add wine to pan, scrape any brown bits from bottom of pan, simmer 2 minutes. Stir liquid into cabbage in saucepan.

4 Spread half cabbage into a casserole, add pork chops in 1 layer, cover with remaining cabbage. Sprinkle with Parmesan and remaining melted butter, bake in a 180°C (350°F) oven until top is golden, about 20 minutes.

Serves 4

Pork Chops with Mustard Cheese Crust

SUCCULENT SEAFOOD

The wonderful thing about seafood is that it is good for us and these sure-fire recipes are guaranteed to please.

Mussels in Garlic and Basil Tomato Sauce

2.5kg (5lb) mussels

5 tblspn olive oil

2 cloves garlic

6 fresh basil leaves

4 ripe tomatoes, peeled, finely chopped

1 Place mussels in a sink filled with cold water. Add ¼ cup salt, mix well. Leave to soak 1 hour.

2 Drain mussels, scrub with a stiff brush under cold running water, pull away beards and discard any open mussels, or any that stay open when tapped.

3 Place mussels in a large pan with 2 tablespoons of the oil. Cover and steam mussels open, shaking the pan. This may be done in batches. Remove mussels from shells. Set meat aside, discard shells, keeping a few for garnish. Strain pan juices, reserve.

4 Combine garlic and basil leaves in a mortar and grind to a paste. Heat remaining oil in a frying pan, add garlic and basil paste. Saute 1 minute, add tomato. Season to taste with salt and freshly ground pepper.

5 Add about ½ cup of the reserved pan juices, simmer until sauce starts to thicken, about 5 minutes, heat through very gently about 8 minutes. Serve hot, garnished with mussel shells.

Serves 4

Mussels Au Gratin

24 mussels, cleaned

1 tblspn fresh basil, chopped

¾ cup freshly grated Parmesan cheese

60g (2oz) butter, melted

1 cup stale breadcrumbs

2 cloves garlic, crushed

1 Combine mussels and 1 cup water in a saucepan, bring to the boil, cook mussels until shells open (about 3 minutes).

2 Remove mussels from water, open shells, discard top shell and loosen mussel meat in shells.

3 In a small bowl combine remaining ingredients, top each mussel with a tablespoon of mixture. Grill for 5 minutes until toppings are golden.

Serves 4

Mussels Au Gratin

Scallops in White Wine

Scallops in White Wine

250g (½lb) pink scallops, shelled

4 tblspn butter

¼ cup white wine

1 cup cream

pinch thyme

2 tblspn chives, finely chopped

1 In a large frypan, melt butter, add scallops. Saute until cooked through, about 3 minutes. Remove scallops with a slotted spoon; set aside.

2 Add wine, cream and thyme to pan, bring to the boil. Reduce heat and simmer 8 minutes until reduced slightly.

3 Add scallops and chives, stir until scallops are covered in sauce. Serve immediately.

Serves 2

Baked Oregano Sardines

1kg (2lb) fresh sardines

½ cup olive oil

¼ cup chopped parsley

2 cloves garlic, finely chopped

¼ tspn dried oregano

2 tblspn red wine vinegar

1 Clean sardines under cold running water, remove bones. Dry thoroughly on paper towels.

2 Brush an ovenproof serving dish with 1 tablespoon of the oil, add sardines in one layer.

3 In a small bowl combine parsley, garlic, oregano and vinegar, mix well. Spread evenly over sardines.

4 Pour over remaining oil, bake in a 180°C (350°F) oven for 20 minutes. Serve hot.

Serves 4

Atlantic Salmon Fillets with Avocado Sauce

4 Atlantic salmon fillets, 185g (6oz) each

⅓ cup olive oil

2 limes, halved

1 avocado, cut into 0.5cm (¼in) cubes

1 bunch chives, chopped

1 Brush salmon fillets with 1 tablespoon oil. Squeeze with juice of 1 lime. Stand at room temperature for 15 minutes.

2 In a bowl combine avocado, remaining olive oil, chives and half remaining lime, freshly squeezed. Season to taste with salt and freshly ground pepper.

3 Line griller tray with foil. Place salmon fillets on foil, skin side down. Season to taste with salt and freshly ground pepper. Grill fish without turning until opaque.

Steamed Gemfish in Radicchio Leaves

4 Serve on heated plates, topped with avocado sauce.

Serves 4

Gravlax (Dill-cured Salmon)

500g (1lb) Atlantic salmon fillets

¼ cup sea salt

¼ cup sugar

6 sprigs of dill

¼ cup brandy

1 Place salmon on a bench skin side down. Season top with salt, sugar and freshly ground white pepper to taste. Place dill sprigs on top, pat all seasonings solidly into the fish.

2 Pour brandy into a dish large enough to hold salmon in one layer. Place salmon into the dish skin side up. Cover dish with plastic wrap, place a 1kg (2lb) weight on top. Refrigerate 3 days.

3 Remove weight and wrap, transfer salmon carefully to a cutting board. Scrape off seasoning. Cut diagonally into 0.5cm (¼ in) slices, discarding skin. Serve as a first course.

Serves 4

Redfish with Mango

4 redfish fillets, 185g (6oz) each

½ cup dry white wine

½ tspn ground bay leaves

1 mango, peeled, sliced

1 Poach redfish fillets in wine until fish flakes when prodded with a fork. Remove fish to a serving platter, keep warm.

2 Add bay leaves and mango to wine, simmer 3 minutes.

3 Arrange mango on top of fillets, pour liquid over. Serve immediately.

Serves 4

Steamed Gemfish in Radicchio Leaves

4 fillets of gemfish

¼ tspn cracked black pepper

1 tspn chopped fresh coriander

½ tspn sambal oelek (or chilli paste)

16 large radicchio leaves

¼ cup fresh lime juice

1 Remove skin from fillets, season, chop into small pieces, place in small bowl. Add pepper, coriander, chilli and lime juice.

2 Divide mixture into 8, place mixture into leaves, wrap 2 leaves around each portion; carefully tie the parcels with cotton.

3 Place parcels in a steamer basket over simmering water, cover and steam for 8 minutes.

Serves 4

Calamari in Chilli Tomato Sauce

1kg (2lb) baby calamari

2 cloves garlic, crushed

¾ cup olive oil

425g (13½oz) can tomatoes, pureed

¼ tspn chilli flakes

¼ cup finely chopped parsley

1 Clean calamari by removing ink sac, mouth, eyes and inner bone. Skin, wash in several changes of cold water, separate sac and tentacles.

2 Saute garlic in half a cup of the oil for 2 minutes, add pureed tomato and chilli flakes. Add salt and freshly ground black pepper to taste. Simmer 12 minutes.

3 Heat remaining oil in a large frying pan. Add calamari and brown all over, turning frequently. Pour sauce over calamari, cover, simmer 1 hour or until calamari is tender.

4 Spoon into a heated serving dish, sprinkle with chopped parsley. Serve hot.

Serves 4

Fried Rainbow Trout and Baby Potatoes

16 baby new potatoes

8 sprigs fresh thyme

4 rainbow trout, about 315g (10oz) each

½ cup unsalted butter

2 tblspn chopped parsley

1 Steam potatoes until just tender, about 10 minutes. Halve and set aside. Place 2 thyme sprigs inside each trout.

2 Heat butter in a large frying pan. When foam starts to subside, add trout. Cook 5 minutes. Turn trout to other side, add halved potatoes.

3 Cook a further 5 minutes, turning potatoes from time to time, until trout is cooked through and potatoes are golden.

4 Season to taste with salt and freshly grated pepper, place on heated plates, sprinkle with parsley. Serve immediately.

Serves 4

Deep-fried Chilli Coconut Prawns (Shrimp)

24 uncooked king prawns (shrimp), peeled (tails left intact) and deveined

3 eggs, lightly beaten

¼ tspn chilli powder

1 cup plain flour

2 cups stale breadcrumbs

1½ cups shredded coconut

1 Combine eggs and chilli powder. Roll each prawn in flour, leaving a thick flour coating on each. Dip prawns into egg mixture, then roll in the combined bread crumbs and coconut.

2 Heat oil in a large, heavy saucepan. Add the prawns and cook for 2 minutes. Drain on absorbent paper.

Serves 4

Whiting with Spinach and Yoghurt Sauce

1 cup tightly packed spinach leaves

¾ cup plain yoghurt

2 spring onions (scallions), coarsely chopped

1 clove garlic, coarsely chopped

1 tinned anchovy fillet

4 whiting fillets, about 185g (6oz) each

1 Combine spinach, yoghurt, spring onion, garlic and anchovy in a food processor. Puree. Season to taste with salt and freshly ground black pepper. Place in a bowl, cover, refrigerate 1 hour.

2 Grill whiting fillets until opaque, turning once. Place on heated plates, spoon over spinach and yoghurt sauce. Serve immediately.

Serves 4

Deep-fried Chilli Coconut Prawns (Shrimp) (top); Marinated Oysters in Bacon

Marinated Oysters in Bacon

2 tblspn soy sauce

1 tblspn honey

½ tspn Worcestershire sauce

4 bacon rashers

12 small wooden skewers

2 dozen oysters, shells discarded

1 In a small bowl combine soy sauce, honey, and Worcestershire sauce and set aside.

2 Cut rind off bacon, and discard. Cut rashers into strips, 3cm (1¼ in) long. Thread skewers with oysters and bacon (two oysters per skewer).

3 Place skewers onto a foil-lined baking tray. Pour marinade over oysters, cover and leave for 30 minutes.

4 Grill oysters until bacon is golden. Serve immediately.

Makes 12

Prawn (Shrimp) and Mozzarella Skewers

24 uncooked king (large) prawns (shrimp)

500g (1lb) mozzarella cheese

425g (13½oz) can peeled tomatoes, undrained, chopped

1 tspn dried oregano, crumbled

1 Shell and devein prawns, pat dry with paper towels. Cut 24 x 2.5cm (1in) cubes of mozzarella. Chop any remaining cheese finely.

2 Thread 4 prawns and 4 mozzarella cubes alternately onto skewers. Place skewers in a greased baking dish. Top with tomatoes and juice. Sprinkle with oregano and remaining mozzarella. Season to taste with salt and freshly ground black pepper.

3 Bake in a 180°C (350°F) oven until cooked through and cheese on top is melted and bubbly. Serve hot.

Serves 6

Ocean Trout with Citrus Ginger Sauce

2 small trout cutlets

30g (1oz) butter

1 tblspn fresh ginger, finely sliced

¼ cup orange juice

1 tblspn brown sugar

1 Heat butter in frying pan. Add trout, cook 3 minutes each side, or until cooked through. Remove trout, leaving fish juices and butter in pan.

2 Add remaining ingredients to pan, cook sauce for 10 minutes, or until slightly thickened. Pour sauce over trout, garnish with strips of lime rind and vegetables if desired.

Serves 2

Snapper with Green Peppercorn Sauce

½ cup bottled clam juice

½ cup dry white wine

1 cup cream

4 snapper fillets, about 185g (6oz) each

⅓ cup unsalted butter

1 tblspn green peppercorns, drained and rinsed

1 Combine clam juice and wine in a small saucepan. Reduce to half a cup over high heat. Add cream, reduce to ⅔ cup. Keep warm.

2 Butter 4 pieces of foil large enough to hold fillets. Place fillets on foil, season to taste with salt, add pieces of butter, fold and seal foil packets securely.

3 Place on a baking sheet and cook in a 200°C (400°F) oven about 12 minutes.

4 When ready to serve add green peppercorns to sauce. Warm through. Remove snapper from foil and place on heated plates. Pour sauce over fish, serve hot.

Serves 4

Ocean Trout with Citrus Ginger Sauce

Ocean Perch Fillets with Pear Sauce

1 tblspn unsalted butter

4 ocean perch fillets, 185g (6oz) each

¼ cup spring onions (scallions), chopped

2 pears, peeled, cored, sliced

¼ cup dry white wine

¼ cup plain yoghurt

1 Melt butter in a frying pan, add fillets, fry gently about 8 minutes, turning once. Remove from pan, keep warm.

2 Add spring onions to frying pan, saute 3 minutes, add pear slices, cook until just tender.

3 Add wine and yoghurt, stir to combine well, heat through gently. Season to taste with salt and freshly ground pepper.

4 Return fillets to pan, reheat gently in sauce. Place fillets onto heated plates, spoon pear sauce over. Serve immediately.

Serves 4

Swordfish Steaks with Mustard Butter

⅓ cup unsalted butter, room temperature

1 tblspn wholegrain mustard

¼ cup finely chopped onion

4 swordfish steaks, about 185g (6oz) each

2 tblspn peanut oil

1 Combine butter, mustard and onion in a bowl, beat to mix well, season to taste with salt and freshly ground pepper.

2 Dry fish with paper towels, brush with 1 tablespoon of the oil. Use remaining oil to brush griller tray.

Bream and Tomato Potage

750g (1½ lb) bream fillets, skinless

2 tblspn chopped parsley

2 large tomatoes, chopped

1 red capsicum (pepper), chopped

1 In a large saucepan add four tablespoons of water, heat and add onions. Sweat onions for 3 minutes.

2 Chop fish fillets into 2cm (¾in) squares, add to the onions. Add lemon juice, tomatoes and capsicum, cook 5 minutes or until fish is cooked through.

3 Add parsley and toss through fish mixture, serve immediately.

Serves 2

Snapper with Lemon Soy Marinade and Caviar

4 snapper fillets

2 tblspn soy sauce

2½ tblspn lemon juice

½ cup cream

¼ tspn ground black pepper

4 tspn red caviar

1 In a small bowl mix soy sauce with ½ lemon juice. Pour mixture over fish fillets, cover and refrigerate 2 hours.

2 Mix remainder of lemon juice with cream, and beat with electric mixer until thickened and soft peaks form.

3 Heat well-seasoned cast-iron frying pan on high heat for about 3 minutes. Remove fish from marinade (reserve marinade juice). Sprinkle pepper on fish fillets and cook fillets until charred and cooked through (approximately 2 minutes each side).

4 Pour reserved marinade over fish and cook a further 30 seconds. Garnish with cream and caviar. Serve with vegetables.

Serves 4

Bream and Tomato Potage (top); Snapper with Lemon Soy Marinade and Caviar

3 Place fish steaks on griller tray and cook under a preheated grill until just done, about 6 minutes, turning once.

4 Place a quarter of the butter mixture on each steak, return briefly to heat under the grill until butter is bubbling. Serve immediately on heated plates.

Serves 4

John Dory Fillets with Curry Sauce

2 tblspn unsalted butter

⅓ cup finely chopped onion

⅓ cup dry vermouth

2 tblspn curry powder

1 tblspn lemon juice

4 John Dory fillets, about 185g (6oz) each

1 Melt butter in a saucepan, add onion. Saute until onion is golden, about 5 minutes.

2 Add vermouth, curry powder, lemon juice and salt to taste. Cook a further 2 minutes.

3 Place fillets into a heatproof dish large enough to hold fish in one layer. Pour over curry sauce. Place dish under a preheated grill, cook about 3 minutes or until fish is done when tested.

4 Place fillets on heated plates, spoon over sauce remaining in dish. Season with freshly ground pepper. Serve immediately.

Serves 4   *recipe-31 pg.6*

VERSATILE EGG AND CHEESE DISHES

Add a few ingredients to these store-cupboard staples and you can come up with stunning meals as these recipes demonstrate.

Swiss Cheese Fondue

1 clove garlic, crushed

500g (1lb) Gruyere cheese, grated

3 tblspn potato flour

¾ cup dry white wine

broccoli heads, blanched

cauliflower heads, blanched

1 Rub around the inside of fondue pot with the crushed garlic. Add cheese, flour and wine.

2 Cook over medium heat until cheese has melted and mixture is a thick consistency.

3 Place vegetables on the end of skewers and dip into cheese.

Serves 4

Roquefort Souffle

4 tblspn butter

3 tblspn plain flour

1 cup milk

100g (3½oz) roquefort cheese, crumbled

2 eggs yolks

7 egg whites

1 In a medium saucepan, melt butter over low heat. Add flour and cook, stirring for 2 minutes.

2 Remove from heat, whisk in the milk, return to the heat, bring to the boil whisking until thickened. Remove sauce from heat, stir in cheese.

3 In a small bowl, whisk about ⅓ cup of the warm cheese sauce into the egg yolks. Whisk the egg yolk mixture back into the cheese sauce. Transfer to a large bowl and cool to room temperature. Loosely cover with plastic wrap.

4 Preheat the oven to 180°C (350°F) and grease a 7-cup capacity souffle dish with butter.

5 In a large bowl, beat egg whites until stiff peaks form. Fold egg whites into cheese sauce mixture until combined. Pour mixture into prepared dish and bake in moderate oven 25 to 30 minutes. Serve immediately.

Serves 4

Swiss Cheese Fondue (left)
Roquefort Souffle (above)

Fresh Peaches Stuffed with Ricotta Cheese

2 yellow slipstone peaches, peeled, halved and stoned

½ cup ricotta cheese

2 bacon rashers, rind removed, chopped finely

1 tblspn fresh chopped chives

1 tblspn freshly grated Parmesan cheese

1 tblspn French dressing

1 Arrange peach halves on serving plate.

2 In a medium bowl combine ricotta cheese, bacon, chives, Parmesan cheese and French dressing, mix well.

3 Spoon mixture into the centre of each half and grill under a low heat for 1 minute. Serve immediately.

Serves 4

Definitive Macaroni and Cheese

250g (½lb) macaroni

¼ cup unsalted butter, cubed

1½ cup full fat milk

500g (1lb) mature cheddar cheese, grated

2 eggs, beaten

2 tspn Dijon mustard

1 Cook macaroni in lightly salted boiling water until just tender. Drain. Place in a large ovenproof dish, toss with butter.

2 Add 1 cup of the milk and about three quarters of the cheese. Mix well.

3 Add beaten eggs and mustard, season to taste with salt and freshly ground pepper. Mix again.

4 Place dish in a 180°C (350°F) oven, cook for 20 minutes, stirring in more cheese every 5 minutes, and more milk if necessary to keep dish moist. Serve hot.

Serves 4

Eggs Florentine (top); Fresh Peaches Stuffed with Ricotta Cheese

Spanish Potato Pie

2 potatoes, peeled

5 tblspn oil

1 onion, finely chopped

8 eggs

1 tspn dried rosemary

1 tblspn chopped chives

1 Chop potatoes into 1cm (½in) cubes. Heat oil in a large frypan, add potatoes and saute, stirring constantly. Cook potatoes for 15 minutes.

2 Add onions and cook a further 15 minutes.

3 Beat eggs with a whisk for 1 minute. Add rosemary and chives, then add potatoes and onions, mix to combine.

4 Pour mixture into a 23cm (9in) ovenproof flan dish, bake in moderate oven 25-30 minutes.

Serves 6

Eggs Florentine

10 spinach leaves, stems removed

4 eggs, hard-boiled, shelled and halved

¾ cup cream

½ tspn potato flour

¼ cup grated cheddar cheese

pinch paprika

1 Bring a large saucepan of water to the boil, blanch spinach for 2 seconds, refresh under cold water, drain.

2 Arrange spinach in a serving dish, top with eggs.

3 In a medium saucepan combine cream and potato flour, heat gently until sauce thickens. Add cheese and stir until melted.

4 Pour sauce over eggs and sprinkle with paprika.

Serves 4

Fettucine Frittata (top); Frittata with Spanish Onion

Frittata with Spanish Onion

½ thinly sliced large Spanish onion

3 tblspn olive oil

4 eggs

60g (2oz) mozzarella, coarsely grated

1 tblspn chopped fresh basil

1 In a frying pan cook onion in 1 tablespoon oil over low heat until soft and golden, about 15 minutes. Season to taste with salt and freshly ground black pepper. Cool.

2 Place eggs in a bowl, beat to blend, season to taste with salt and freshly ground pepper. Add cooled onion, mozzarella and basil. Mix well.

3 Heat 2 tablespoons of the oil in a frying pan over medium heat. Pour in the egg mixture, tilt pan to distribute mixture evenly. Cook until bottom is golden brown and eggs are still runny on top, about 7 minutes.

4 Place pan under a heated grill, cook until top is golden, about 4 minutes. Slide frittata onto a heated plate. Serve warm or at room temperature, cut into wedges.

Serves 4

Deep-fried Pecorino Meringues

4 egg whites

250g (½lb) very finely grated Pecorino cheese

1/8 tspn chilli powder

1 cup flour

2 eggs, beaten

1 cup breadcrumbs

1 Beat egg whites with a pinch of salt until very stiff. Add cheese and chilli powder, fold in thoroughly. Shape into walnut-sized balls.

2 Place flour in a deep plate, season with salt and freshly ground pepper. Coat balls with flour, shake off excess, dip in egg, coat with breadcrumbs. Refrigerate 1 hour.

3 Deep-fry in hot oil in batches until golden. Drain on paper towels, keep warm. Serve hot.

Serves 4

Fettucine Frittata

1 cup milk

1 cup cream

6 eggs, lightly beaten

2 tblspn chopped parsley

1 red capsicum (pepper), chopped

200g (6½oz) fettucini

1 Whisk milk and cream into eggs, stir in parsley and capsicum.

2 Cook fettucine in boiling water until tender, about 8 minutes; drain.

3 Stir fettucine into eggs and cream mixture and pour mixture into a greased 23cm (9in) flan dish. Bake in moderate oven 25-30 minutes.

Serves 4

Maharajah's Scrambled Eggs

2 tblspn ghee or peanut oil

1 small onion, finely chopped

½ tspn cumin powder

1/8 tspn cayenne powder

4 large eggs, lightly beaten

1 tblspn chopped fresh coriander

1 Heat ghee or oil in a frying pan, add onion, cook until golden, about 3 minutes. Add cumin, cayenne and salt to taste, stir over heat to combine for 30 seconds.

2 Add eggs, cook over medium low heat, stirring constantly, until eggs have set. Remove from heat immediately, divide among 2 heated plates. Sprinkle with coriander.

Serves 2

YOUR 'SIX INGREDIENT' STORE CUPBOARD

Of course, you'll need more than just six ingredients to prove to yourself how much simpler cooking really can be.

So it's a good idea to stock up your kitchen cupboard with some of the staple ingredients that you'll need. If you follow this shopping list, you'll find you'll always have the necessary ingredients to hand. And if you buy progressively you'll hardly even notice the effect on your weekly shopping bill.

Breads and Grains

Bread — wholemeal, pita, French, Italian
Breadcrumbs
Biscuits for cheese
Corn chips for dips
Flour — plain, self-rising, wholemeal
Pasta and noodles — spaghetti, fettucini, macaroni, spinach, pasta, egg noodles
Rice — plain, Basmati, Arborio
Tortillas
Poppadoms

Sauces and Condiments

Ketchup
Chilli sauce
Tabasco sauce
Angostura bitters
Mayonnaise
Mustard, dry and prepared
Horseradish
Olive oil
Vegetable oil, such as peanut or safflower oil
Vinaigrette
Soy sauce
Tamari
Peeled Italian tomatoes
Tomato paste
Chicken and beef stock cubes
Vinegar, white, red wine, white wine, tarragon and cider
Worcestershire sauce
Sun-dried tomatoes
Herbs and spices
Curry powder
Chutney
Gherkins

Frozen Foods

Home-made stocks
Fresh breadcrumbs
Peas
Butter
Margarine
Filo dough
Puff pastry
Bread rolls
Orange juice concentrate

Canned Foods

Crabmeat
Salmon
Prawns (shrimp)
Tuna
Artichoke hearts
Bamboo shoots
Hearts of palm
Beans
Olives
Water chestnuts

For Baking

Sugar — granulated, brown, powdered
Corn syrup
Maple syrup
Jam, jelly, preserves
Desiccated coconut
Unsweetened cocoa powder
Instant coffee powder
Choc Bits
Raisins
Nuts — almonds, pecans, peanuts, walnuts
Oil — vegetable, peanut
Vegetable shortening (copha)
Gelatine
Bi-carbonate of soda
Baking soda
Baking powder

Wines and Spirits

Brandy
Coffee Liqueur
Dry red wine
Dry white wine
Orange liqueur (Grand Marnier, Cointreau)
Rum
Sherry
Vermouth
Vodka

Cheeses

Cheddar
Parmesan
Gruyere
Blue-vein cheese
Camembert
Brie
Cream Cheese

SIX SUPER MENUS

Cooking for special occasions has never been simpler. We have selected great dishes that go well together, yet with no recipe that uses more than six ingredients. Feast your eyes and your guests on the pages that follow.

Menu 1

Spaghetti with Corn and Coriander Sauce

Fish Fillets with Prosciutto and Sun-dried Tomato Topping

Warm Capsicum (Pepper) Salad with Fresh Herbs

Rockmelon (Cantaloupe) Sorbet with Port

Menu 2

Salmon and Caviar Spread

Pork Chops with Rosemary Sauce

Cherry Tomato and Basil Salad

Cold Cucumber and Egg Fettucini Salad

Mixed Berry Summer Pudding

Menu 3

Smoked Trout Timbales with Tomato Basil Sauce

Chicken Fillets with Apples and Brandy Sauce

Julienne Vegetables with Lemon Dressing

Mixed Berry and Brandy Cream Tarts

Menu 4

Watercress Soup with Orange

Spicy Baked Nugget Pumpkin

Lamb Shanks with Brussel Sprouts and Turnips

Apple Flan with Apricot Calvados Glaze

Menu 5

Asparagus Mousse with Tomato Sauce

Watercress and Orange Salad

Roast Beef with Squash and Thyme

Fluffy Chocolate Mousse

Menu 6

Deep-fried White Bait with Tartar Sauce

Veal Strips with Capsicum (Pepper) and Mustard Dressing

Beans in Curry Cream

Garlic Roast Potatoes with Walnuts

Vanilla Cream Ring with Strawberries

Spaghetti with Corn and Coriander Sauce

2 medium tomatoes

⅔ cups cooked corn kernels

250g (½lb) dry spaghetti

1 egg

1 tblspn red wine vinegar

½ cup freshly chopped coriander

1 Peel and seed tomatoes, cut into small dice.

2 Bring a large saucepan of water to the boil, add spaghetti and cook until just tender; drain.

3 In a food processor or blender process egg until light and fluffy, add half of the diced tomato and vinegar, process a further 1 minute.

4 Add corn and tomato-egg mixture to spaghetti, add coriander and remaining tomato, toss well to coat. Serve immediately.

Serves 4

Spaghetti with Corn and Coriander Sauce

Fish Fillets with Prosciutto and Sun-dried Tomato Topping

2 tblspn olive oil

60g (2oz) thinly sliced prosciutto, cut into strips

4 fillets of boneless white fish

1 cup sun-dried tomatoes, chopped

¼ cup finely chopped spring onion (scallion)

1 Heat oil in large frying pan, add prosciutto and stir until heated through. Transfer prosciutto to a small bowl with a slotted spoon and set aside.

2 Add fish to frying pan and cook until opaque, approximately 2 minutes each side. Transfer to a warm plate, cover with foil.

3 Add tomatoes and prosciutto to frying pan, cook over medium heat for 5 minutes. Stir in spring onions and serve over fish.

Serves 4

Fish Fillets with Prosciutto and Sun-dried Tomato Topping (top); Warm Capsicum (Pepper) Salad with Fresh Herbs

Warm Capsicum (Pepper) Salad with Fresh Herbs

¼ cup olive oil

1 red onion, thinly sliced

4 capsicum (peppers), red and green, cut into strips

⅓ cup fresh chopped parsley

⅓ cup fresh chopped basil

¼ cup red wine vinegar

1 In a large frying pan heat the oil. Add onion and capsicum, cover and cook over medium heat for 10 minutes or until capsicum are softened.

2 Add parsley and basil, cook for another 5 minutes.

3 Stir in vinegar and cook 2 minutes. Season with salt and black pepper if desired.

Serves 8

Rockmelon (Cataloupe) Sorbet with Port

Rockmelon (Cantaloupe) Sorbet with Port

1 large rockmelon (cantaloupe)

½ cup sugar

1 vanilla bean

1 tblspn lime juice

1 tblspn lemon juice

¼ cup port, chilled

1 Peel and seed rockmelon, cut into chunks. In a food processor or blender, process rockmelon to a puree. Push mixture through sieve to remove any lumps.

2 Pour 3 cups of rockmelon puree into a medium saucepan. Add the sugar and vanilla bean to saucepan. Slowly bring mixture to the boil, stirring just until sugar is dissolved. Boil mixture for 5 minutes and remove vanilla bean.

3 Add lime and lemon juice, mix well. Pour mixture into a foil-lined tin and freeze for 2 hours.

4 Remove from freezer and break ice with a fork, stirring until mixture becomes mushy. Return to freezer and freeze another 2 hours.

5 Break up ice with fork and return to freezer until ready to serve. Scoop sorbet into individual glasses and pour 2 tablespoons of port on top of sorbet.

Note: This recipe can also be made in a ice-cream machine. Freeze according to manufacturers instructions.

Makes about 3 cups

Salmon and Caviar Spread

Salmon and Caviar Spread

2 medium salmon steaks

1 cup chicken stock

100g (3½oz) smoked salmon, chopped

200g (6½oz) unsalted butter

1 tblspn lemon juice

2 tblspn red caviar

1 In a small frying pan bring stock to the boil over medium heat. Reduce to a simmer and add salmon. Cover and poach for about 5 minutes or until cooked through. Remove salmon and allow to cool.

2 Flake salmon, discarding skin and bones. In a food processor or blender, process smoked salmon with butter and lemon juice until smooth.

3 Carefully stir in flaked salmon until well combined, then stir in caviar. Serve at room temperature with toast.

Serves 6

55

Pork Chops with Rosemary Sauce

8 centre-cut loin pork chops, 2cm (1in) thick

cracked black pepper

4 tblspn butter

2 tblspn walnut oil

1 tblspn fresh rosemary, chopped

1 cup red wine

1 Remove any excess fat from chops, sprinkle with black pepper.

2 Melt 1 tablespoon of the butter in a frying pan until bubbling. Add the walnut oil and heat with the butter. Add the pork and fry until lightly golden on each side, approximately 3 minutes each side.

3 Sprinkle rosemary over the pork chops and cook a further 1 minute. Transfer pork to a warm oven.

4 Pour the wine into frying pan, scraping up any browned bits from the bottom of the pan, until reduced by half.

5 Stir in remaining 3 tablespoons of butter, pour over pork chops. Serve with vegetables and garnish with fresh rosemary if desired.

Serves 4

Pork Chops with Rosemary Sauce

Cherry Tomato and Basil Salad

2 tblspn olive oil

1 garlic clove, crushed

½ cup sliced bacon, cut into strips

1 tspn red wine vinegar

2 cups cherry tomatoes, halved

⅓ cup finely chopped basil

1 Heat oil in a medium frying pan. Add garlic and bacon, cook for 3 minutes. Remove from heat.

2 Add red wine vinegar, tomatoes and basil, mix well. Serve chilled.

Serves 4

Cold Cucumber and Egg Fettucini Salad

3 Lebanese cucumbers

2 tblspn sesame oil

2 eggs, lightly beaten

2 tblspn red wine vinegar

3 tspn Dijon mustard

⅓ cup chopped leg ham

1 Using a vegetable peeler, peel off slices of cucumber on two sides, discard inside core and seeds.

2 Place cucumber in a colander, sprinkle with salt, set aside for 30 minutes. Rinse cucumber under cold water.

3 Brush a medium frying pan with sesame oil and heat. Pour in half the beaten egg mixture, swirl to cover pan and cook for 2 minutes.

4 Turn omelette with a spatula and cook 1 minute. Repeat with remaining egg mixture. Roll up omelettes and cut into ½cm (¼in) thick strips.

5 Carefully mix cucumber, egg strips and ham together, pour over combined vinegar and mustard. Decorate with cracked black pepper if desired.

Serves 4

Cold Cucumber and Egg Fettucine Salad (top); Cherry Tomato and Basil Salad

Mixed Berry Summer Pudding

Mixed Berry Summer Pudding

8 slices white bread, crusts removed

250g (½lb) blackcurrants

250g (½lb) redcurrants

500g (1lb) raspberries

150g castor sugar

2 tblspn lemon juice

1 Line a 6-cup capacity pudding basin with the bread, reserving some to cover the top.

2 Place the fruit in a medium saucepan with 2 tablespoons of water and the sugar and lemon juice. Cook until blackcurrant skins start to burst, approximately 5 minutes. Remove from heat, cool for 3 minutes.

3 Spoon the fruit into the bread lined basin and top with the reserved bread. Put a plate on top of basin and press down with a weight.

4 Any juice that may be squeezed out, reserve. Store pudding in refrigerator over night.

5 Turn out pudding into a serving plate, pour over reserved juice and decorate with fresh berries and mint if desired.

Serves 6

Menu 3

*Smoked Trout Timbales with
Tomato Basil Sauce*

*Chicken Fillets with Apples
and Brandy Sauce*

*Julienne Vegetables with
Lemon Dressing*

*Mixed Berry and Brandy
Cream Tarts*

Smoked Trout Timbales with Tomato Basil Sauce

400g (13oz) smoked trout

500g (1lb) cream cheese, softened

2 tblspn lemon juice

¼ cup chopped fresh basil

2 tblspn chopped basil, extra

¾ cup tomato puree

1 tspn tomato paste

1 Line the base and sides of each of 6 half cup timbale tins with a layer of smoked trout; trim edges.

2 In a blender or food processor, combine cream cheese with the lemon juice, ¼ cup basil and remaining smoked trout until smooth. Pack this mixture into each timbale, cover and refrigerate for 2 hours.

3 In a small bowl mix together the tomato puree, tomato paste and extra chopped basil.

4 Gently loosen each timbale with a knife and turn onto serving plate. Pour a little sauce around the base and garnish with a sprig of basil if desired.

Serves 6

Smoked Trout Timbales with Tomato Basil Sauce

Chicken Fillets with Apples and Brandy Sauce

4 tblspn butter

4 chicken breast fillets

1 green apple

1 tblspn chopped shallots

3 tblspn brandy

¾ cup cream

1 Heat 2 tablespoons of butter in a frying pan and saute chicken over medium heat until golden brown, approximately 3 minutes each side.

2 Peel, quarter and core apple, cut into 12 slices. Add the remaining 2 tablespoons of butter to the frying pan and add apple slices. Cook until apples begin to soften.

3 Add the brandy and shallots, turn heat to high and cook for 2 minutes.

4 Remove apples with a slotted spoon and add cream to frying pan. Reduce heat and simmer over medium heat until sauce thickens slightly. Place apples on top of chicken and pour over sauce.

Serves 4

Chicken Fillets with Apples and Brandy Sauce (top); Julienne Vegetables with Lemon Dressing

Julienne Vegetables with Lemon Dressing

4 small beets, root ends removed

2 medium leeks

4 medium zucchini (courgette)

1 radicchio lettuce

3 tblspn lemon juice

2 tblspn olive oil

1 Bring a medium saucepan of water to the boil, add beets and cook until fork tender. Drain and cool to room temperature. Peel beets and cut into julienne strips.

2 Wash leeks and cook in boiling water until tender, drain and cut into julienne strips.

3 Cook zucchini in boiling water, until just cooked, drain. Cool to room temperature, cut into julienne strips.

4 Arrange lettuce leaves on serving plate and arrange clusters of beets, leeks and zucchini strips on top of lettuce.

5 Dress with combined lemon juice and olive oil. Garnish with fresh dill if desired.

Serves 4

Mixed Berry and Brandy Cream Tarts

Mixed Berry and Brandy Cream Tarts

¾ cup cream

1 tblspn brandy

1 tblspn icing sugar

1 packet frozen shortcrust pastry, thawed

¼ cup redcurrants

¾ cup blueberries

1 Beat cream with brandy and icing sugar with an electric mixer until soft peaks form, refrigerate.

2 Cut out 2 rounds of pastry using an 8cm (3in) cutter. Line individual flan tins with removable bases with the pastry and bake in a moderately hot oven for 10 minutes.

3 Leave pastry cases to cool, remove from flan tins.

4 When pastry cases are cold, spoon 2 tablespoons brandy cream into each case and top with berries. Decorate with a mint leaf if desired.

Serves 6

Watercress Soup with Orange

Watercress Soup with Orange

3 cups chicken stock

1 large potato, peeled and chopped

1 bunch watercress

1 cup unsweetened orange juice

¾ cup cream

1 orange, segmented, for garnish

1 Bring chicken stock to the boil, add potato and cook until tender. Add watercress to stock, cover and cook for 3 minutes.

2 Place stock, potato and watercress into a blender or food processor and blend for 2 minutes. Add the cream and orange juice, then blend for 2-3 seconds.

3 Return to the saucepan and slowly reheat, being careful not to boil.

4 Serve soup hot, garnished with orange segments and a sprig of watercress if desired.

Serves 4-6

Spicy Baked Nugget Pumpkin

2 golden nugget pumpkins

2 tblspn honey

1 tblspn maple syrup

1 tblspn butter

2 tblspn sultanas

1 tspn mixed spice

1 Peel pumpkins and remove seeds, cut into 1cm (½in) slices.

2 In a small saucepan, combine honey, maple syrup, butter, sultanas and spice. Gently stir over a medium heat until runny, approximately 3 minutes.

3 Place pumpkin into a baking dish and brush with honey spice marinade, pour any excess into baking dish.

4 Bake pumpkin a moderate oven 35-40 minutes turning frequently.

Serves 4

*Spicy Baked Nugget Pumpkin (top);
Lamb Shanks with Brussel Sprouts and Turnips*

Lamb Shanks with Brussel Sprouts and Turnips

4 trimmed lamb shanks

2 clove garlic, crushed

½ cup dry vermouth

1 tspn fresh chopped thyme

2 large turnips, peeled and sliced

1 cup small brussel sprouts

1 Grill lamb shanks, turning frequently until well-browned on all sides, approximately 25 minutes. Place lamb shanks in an ovenproof baking dish.

2 Add the garlic, vermouth, thyme and 1 cup of water. Bake uncovered for 40 minutes.

3 Add the turnips and brussel sprouts and bake a further 20 minutes.

4 Remove meat from the bone and keep warm in a baking dish in the oven. Remove turnips and brussel sprouts with a slotted spoon, add to meat.

5 Strain remaining meat juices through a sieve and pour over meat and vegetables.

Serves 4

Apple Flan with Apricot Calvados Glaze

1 cup plain flour

¼ cup cornflour

155g (5oz) butter, chopped

3 medium apples, peeled, cored and sliced

½ cup apricot jam

2 tblspn Calvados brandy

1 Using fingertips, mix together flour, cornflour and butter until mixture resembles fine breadcrumbs. Mix in enough cold a water to form a dough.

2 Knead dough lightly, wrap and refrigerate for half an hour. Roll dough to fit a 23cm (9in) flan tin. Bake blind for 15 minutes in a moderately hot oven.

3 Arrange an overlapping layer of apples in pastry case. In a medium saucepan melt jam with the brandy over a low heat.

4 Brush apples with jam mixture and bake in a moderate oven 30-35 minutes. Serve hot or cold with cream and strawberries if desired.

Serves 4-6

Apple Flan with Apricot Calvados Glaze

Asparagus Mousse with Tomato Sauce

1 cup tinned asparagus spears, chopped and drained

2 eggs

¼ tspn nutmeg

¼ tspn chopped fresh basil

2 tblspn sour cream

1 tin peeled tomatoes, drained

1 Puree asparagus in a food processor or blender until smooth. While motor is running, add eggs, cream, nutmeg and basil, process for 30 seconds.

2 Lightly grease four quarter-cup capacity ramekins and divide asparagus puree between each.

3 Place ramekins in a baking dish, with 2cm (¾in) of hot water. Cover baking dish with foil and bake in moderate oven for 30 minutes.

4 Remove seeds from tomatoes and puree tomatoes in a blender or food processor until smooth, spoon 2 teaspoons of sauce onto each serving plate.

5 Unmould mousse next to sauce and garnish with asparagus spears.

Serves 4

Asparagus Mousse with Tomato Sauce

Watercress and Orange Salad

1 clove garlic, crushed

2 tblspn fresh orange juice

2 tblspn olive oil

1 bunch watercress

2 navel oranges, segmented

12 black olives

1 In a small bowl combine garlic, orange juice and oil, whisk until combined.

2 On a serving dish arrange a bed of watercress. Place orange segments and olives on top and pour dressing just before serving.

Serves 4

Watercress and Orange Salad (top);
Roast Beef with Squash and Thyme

Roast Beef with Squash and Thyme

1½kg beef rib roast, boned and rolled

3 tblspn butter

1 tblspn cracked black pepper

1 tspn dried cardamon

2 tblspn chopped fresh thyme

375g (¾lb) baby squash, cut into halves

1 Cook beef in a large baking dish with the butter in a moderae oven for 30 minutes. Remove baking dish from oven.

2 Sprinkle beef with cracked pepper, cardamon and thyme. Add squash to baking dish and toss in pan juices.

3 Bake for a further 20 minutes. Slice beef and pour over pan juices. Serve immediately with squash.

Serves 4

Fluffy Chocolate Mousse

60g (2oz) butter

100g (3½oz) dark chocolate

3 eggs, separated

1 tspn orange rind

1 tblspn Tia Maria

2 tblspn cream, whipped

1 Melt the butter with the chocolate over a double saucepan, stirring constantly. Cool to room temperature, stir in orange rind and Tia Maria.

2 Beat egg yolks with ¼ cup warm water in an electric mixer until light and fluffy, approximately 5 minutes. Fold egg mixture into chocolate mixture until combined.

3 Beat egg whites with sugar until stiff. Fold egg white mixture into chocolate mixture and pour into 4 serving glasses and refrigerate for 2 hours. Decorate with cream.

Serves 4

Fluffy Chocolate Mousse

Deep-fried White Bait with Tartar Sauce

Deep-fried White Bait with Tartar Sauce

500g (1lb) white bait

¼ cup potato flour

¾ cup plain flour

pinch paprika

2 cups oil for frying

½ cup tartar sauce

1 Wash white bait and drain.

2 In a large bowl combine potato flour, plain flour and paprika. Whisk in ¾ cup cold water; keep whisking until smooth.

3 Add white bait to batter.

4 Heat oil in a medium saucepan over medium heat for 5 minutes. Add white bait to oil four at a time. Fry until golden.

5 Serve with tartar sauce and garnish with lemon and parsley if desired.

Serves 4

Veal Strips with Capsicum (Pepper) and Mustard Dressing

3 tblspn olive oil
500g (1lb) veal fillet, cut into strips
1 red capsicum (pepper), seeded and sliced into strips
2 tblspn Dijon mustard
1 tblspn chopped parsley
8 assorted lettuce leaves

1 Heat oil in a large frying pan over medium heat. Add veal and capsicum, cook, stirring constantly, for 4 minutes.

2 Remove veal and capsicum with a slotted spoon and keep warm in oven.

3 Add the mustard to the pan and ¼ cup water, bring to the boil, cook 30 seconds. Remove from heat and stir in parsley.

4 Return veal and capsicum to pan and coat in mustard dressing.

5 Arrange lettuce leaves in a serving bowl, add veal and capsicum, toss gently.

Serves 4

Veal Strips with Capsicum (Pepper) and Mustard Dressing

Beans in Curry Cream

4 tblspn butter

½ cup slivered almonds

1 tblspn mild curry powder

1 red onion, chopped

500g (1lb) green beans, tops removed, cut in halves

¾ cups sour cream

1 In a medium frying pan melt 2 tablespoons butter over medium heat. Add the almonds and curry powder and cook for 4 minutes, stirring constantly.

2 Remove almonds, add remaining butter to pan. Add onion and beans, cook for 3 minutes, stirring constantly.

3 Remove bean and onions from pan. Add cream to the pan, bring to the boil, reduce heat and simmer for 3 minutes or until sauce thickens slightly.

4 Add sauce to almonds, onions and beans, toss well.

Serves 4

Beans in Curry Cream (top); Garlic Roast Potatoes with Walnuts

Garlic Roast Potatoes with Walnuts

10 new potatoes, peeled and quartered

4 tblspn olive oil

1 tblspn ground pepper

3 large cloves garlic, crushed

1½ cup roughly chopped walnuts

1 tblspn finely chopped parsley

1 In a large roasting pan toss together the potatoes, olive oil, pepper, garlic and walnuts.

2 Roast potatoes in a moderate oven for 1 hour. Toss potatoes every 15 minutes. Add the parley and mix well.

Serves 6

Vanilla Cream Ring with Strawberries

Vanilla Cream Ring with Strawberries

1 cup cream

¾ cup icing sugar

1½ envelopes gelatine, plain

2½ cups sour cream

1 tblspn vanilla essence

1 punnet of fresh strawberries

1 Heat cream in small saucepan until warm. Add the sugar and stir until dissolved, do not boil. Remove from the heat and set aside.

2 In a separate saucepan, dissolve the gelatine in ⅓ cup of cold water. Slowly bring gelatine to the boil, stirring constantly, remove from heat.

3 Stir gelatine into cream mixture. Slowly pour the cream gelatine mixture into the sour cream, while stirring.

4 Add vanilla essence and beat mixture in an electric mixer on a low speed, until smooth.

5 Pour the cream mixture into an ungreased 4-cup capacity ring mould and refrigerate 6 hours or until firm.

6 Unmould the vanilla ring onto a serving plate and fill centre with fresh strawberries.

Serves 4-6

TIME SAVING IDEAS
IN THE KITCHEN

These tried and true suggestions will often come in handy when you're in a hurry.

1 To thaw frozen poultry: To avoid the danger of contamination, never defrost poultry at room temperature. Either defrost in the refrigerator, or place in the original wrapping in the sink with cold water to cover. Refresh the water every 30 minutes. This way a 2kg (4lb) chicken will be defrosted in 2 hours.

2 To make quick chilled salads: Store all ingredients like canned fruits, vegetables and meats in the refrigerator at least 24 hours before making a salad. At a pinch, you can place ingredients in the freezer, but no longer than 30 minutes!

3 When a recipe calls for "canned peeled tomatoes, chopped", simply remove the lid, place a pair of scissors in the can, and snip away. This way you can use the whole contents of the can, or drain the "chopped" tomato pieces. The same method can be applied to chopping fresh herbs. Just place herbs in a measuring jug.

4 To make an extra-quick cheese sauce to add some sparkle to plain vegetables: Simply stir some cheese spread or cream cheese into hot vegetables. Cook over gentle heat until heated through and vegetables are coated.

5 To store leftovers: We all have the best of intentions when it comes to leftovers, but how often do we come across some leftover chicken, sausage or vegetables that have been sitting in the fridge for ages and definitely past it? Set aside one area of your refrigerator especially for leftovers, even better, buy a brightly coloured plastic basket for this purpose. So next time someone in the family is looking for a sandwich filling or a little nibble, they'll know exactly where to find it.

POULTRY TO PLEASE

Combining herbs or fruit with poultry creates mouthwatering dishes. Try these irresistible recipes and see what we mean.

Chicken Breast Mediterranean

1 tblspn yellow mustard seeds

1½ cups cream

2 tblspn Dijon mustard

4 whole chicken breasts, bone removed, skin left on

2 tspn freshly squeezed lemon juice

3 spring onions (scallions), thinly sliced

1 In a small frying pan toast mustard seeds over medium high heat, shaking pan, until light brown and starting to pop. Remove to a plate immediately, cool.

2 Place cream in a small saucepan, bring to a boil, reduce heat, cook, stirring from time to time, until cream is thickening and reduced to about 1 cup.

3 Remove from heat, stir in Dijon mustard. Season to taste with salt and freshly ground pepper. Set aside.

4 Season chicken breasts with salt and freshly ground black pepper. Place skin side up in a shallow roasting pan. Cook on the highest level in a 250°C (500°F) oven for 12 minutes.

5 Place pan under a preheated griller, cook until skin is crispy and golden brown.

6 Gently reheat sauce, add lemon juice, spring onions and mustard seeds. Place chicken breasts on heated plates, spoon sauce over.

Serves 4

Bacon Wrapped Spatchcock with Herb Marinade

2 spatchcocks

2 sprigs fresh thyme

1 tblspn dried mixed herbs

3 tblspn melted butter

3 tblspn oil

2 rashers of bacon, rind removed

1 Wash spatchcocks and fill each city with a sprig of thyme.

2 In a small bowl combine herbs, butter and oil. Brush spatchcocks generously with herb butter mixture.

3 Wrap bacon around spatchcocks and secure with a skewer or toothpick.

4 Bake in a moderate oven 30-35 minutes or until cooked through, basting regularly with any remaining herb butter marinade.

5 Serve with baked pumpkin and garnish with fresh herbs if desired.

Serves 4

Bacon Wrapped Spatchcock with Herb Marinade

Creamy Basil-scented Chicken

625g (1¼lb) boned, skinned chicken breasts

¼ cup tightly packed basil leaves

1 clove garlic

2 tblspn olive oil

2 tblspn white wine vinegar

½ cup cream

1 Place chicken breasts between layers of plastic wrap, pound to a ¼cm (1/8in) thickness.

2 Place basil in a processor, mince. With machine running drop garlic through feed tube. Mince. Add oil, season to taste with salt, mix well.

3 Brush one side of chicken pieces with basil-flavoured oil. Place in a preheated frying pan, brush top with oil. Cook under side for barely 1 minute, turn, cook other side. This may be best done in batches. Remove, keep warm.

4 Pour vinegar into pan. Cook over medium high heat, scraping up any browned bits. Add cream and any accumulated juices in chicken platter. Stir until mixture coats the back of a spoon, about 3 minutes. Season to taste with salt and freshly ground pepper. Spoon over chicken. Serve hot.

Serves 4

Dijon Dill Chicken

1.5kg (3lb) chicken pieces

¼ cup chopped fresh dill

⅓ cup unsalted butter

¼ cup Dijon mustard

1 Rinse chicken pieces. Dry thoroughly with paper towels. Rub dill into chicken pieces. Season with freshly ground pepper.

2 Melt butter, remove from heat, add mustard, mix well.

3 Arrange chicken pieces skin-side down in a baking dish large enough to hold chicken in one layer. Spread top with half of the mustard-butter mixture.

4 Bake in a 180°C (350°F) oven for 25 minutes. Turn chicken pieces, spread skin side with remaining mustard butter. Bake a further 30 minutes, or until golden. Serve hot.

Serves 4

Curried Chicken Wings with Mushrooms

4 tblspn butter

8 chicken wings each broken into two pieces

500g (1lb) button mushrooms, sliced

1 cup cream

2 tspn mild curry

1 tblspn chopped fresh coriander

1 In a medium frying pan, melt butter over medium heat until sizzling. Add the chicken wing pieces and cook for 15 minutes, stirring frequently. Remove chicken and keep warm in oven.

2 Add mushrooms to frying pan and cook for 3 minutes. Add the cream and curry powder and bring mixture to the boil. Reduce heat and simmer 10 minutes or until sauce has thickened slightly.

3 Add coriander and chicken pieces, mix well. Serve immediately.

Serves 4

Hazelnut Chicken

½ cup hazelnuts

4 chicken breasts, bone and skin removed

3 tblspn butter

½ cup dry white wine

1 cup cream

1 tspn freshly squeezed lemon juice

1 Place hazelnuts in a shallow baking dish, bake in a 160°C (325°F) oven 12 minutes. Cool, rub off skin, chop.

Curried Chicken Wings with Mushrooms (top); Chicken Drumsticks with Mango Sauce

2 Place chicken breasts between layers of plastic wrap, pound until about 1cm (½in) thick. Season to taste with salt and freshly ground pepper.

3 Heat butter in a frying pan, add chicken breasts, saute until golden all over, about 8 minutes, turning once. Remove, keep warm.

4 Add wine to pan, cook over high heat, scraping up any browned bits. Reduce to 2 tablespoons. Add cream, cook, stirring constantly until slightly thickened. Add lemon juice, season to taste with salt and freshly ground pepper.

5 Place chicken onto heated plates, pour over sauce, sprinkle with toasted hazelnuts.

Serves 4

Chicken Drumsticks with Mango Sauce

8 chicken drumsticks

4 tblspn butter

425g (13½oz) can mango slices

¼ cup thickened cream

¼ tspn nutmeg

1 Melt butter in a large frying pan, add drumsticks, cook for 2 minutes, stirring frequently to avoid sticking.

2 Remove drumsticks from frying pan, place into a baking dish, bake in moderate oven 15-20 minutes or until cooked through.

3 Strain mango slices, reserving mango juice. Add the mango juice to the frying pan. Stir over medium heat until juice boils and thickens slightly. Remove from heat, strain and return sauce to frying pan.

4 Add cream and nutmeg and slowly bring to the boil, reduce heat, simmer 8 minutes. Add the mango slices to sauce and serve with drumsticks.

Serves 4

Chicken Pieces and Apricot Sauce

Chicken Pieces and Apricot Sauce

2 medium uncooked chickens

4 tblspn oil

425g (13½oz) can apricot halves, drained, reserve juice

⅓ cup sugar

3 cups cooked white rice

2 tblspn finely chopped parsley

1 Break chicken into serving pieces and place in a baking dish. Brush chicken with oil and bake in moderate oven until golden brown, approximately 35 minutes.

2 In a saucepan bring the reserved apricot juice and sugar to the boil. Reduce heat and simmer 20 minutes. Add apricot pieces and set aside.

3 Combine parsley with the rice and arrange on the bottom of serving dish. Place baked chicken pieces on top of rice and pour apricot sauce over the top.

Serves 4

Oven-baked Chicken and Potatoes with Lemon and Rosemary

3 tblspn olive oil

4 potatoes, peeled, cut into 4cm (1½in) cubes

1.5kg (3lb) chicken, cut into serving pieces

1 clove garlic, crushed

1 sprig rosemary, chopped

½ cup freshly squeezed lemon juice

1 Use a little of the oil to grease a baking dish large enough to hold chicken and potatoes in one layer. Toss chicken and potatoes in remaining oil, arrange in dish.

2 Sprinkle with garlic, rosemary and ⅓ cup of the lemon juice. Cover with foil. Bake in a 200°C (400°F) oven for 30 minutes, uncover, bake a further 15 minutes, turning chicken and potato from time to time to brown evenly.

3 Serve chicken and potatoes on heated plates, sprinkle with remaining lemon juice. Season to taste with salt and freshly ground pepper. Spoon over pan juices.

Serves 4

Champagne Chicken

1 x 1.5kg (3lb) chicken

⅓ cup champagne

100ml (3fl oz) cream

½ tspn crumbled tarragon

1 large egg yolk

1 Place chicken on a tray in a roasting pan. Cook in a 220°C (425°F) oven until done. Cut into 4 equal serving pieces, set aside.

Minted Glaze Duck

2 Pour off any excess fat from roasting pan, deglaze pan with champagne, scraping bottom of pan to incorporate any browned bits. Add cream and tarragon. Return chicken to pan, season to taste with salt and freshly ground pepper. Keep warm.

3 Place chicken on heated plates. Add a little of the hot sauce to the egg yolk, mix well, return to pan. Stir over low heat until sauce thickens, pour over chicken. Serve hot.

Serves 4

Minted Glaze Duck

1 medium duck

2 tblspn butter

½ cup redcurrant jelly

¼ cup creme de menthe

2 onions, peeled and halved

1 bunch fresh mint

1 Wash duck and trim excess fat away from neck.

2 In a small saucepan, melt butter and redcurrant jelly over medium heat. Add creme de menthe, bring to the boil, simmer 2 minutes; remove from heat.

3 Place onion halves inside cavity of duck with the bunch of mint. Close up cavity with skewers. Place duck in baking dish and brush generously with jelly/mint glaze.

4 Bake in moderate oven for 1 hour, turning duck twice while cooking. Serve with vegetables if desired, garnish with fresh mint.

Serves 2

Vine-wrapped Quail

8 quail, cleaned, giblets removed

8 slices bacon

¼ cup unsalted butter, melted

8 large vine leaves

½ cup brandy

chicken broth

1 Season quail inside and out with salt and freshly ground pepper. Wrap each quail in a slice of bacon. Tie securely with string.

2 Place in a roasting pan, brush with melted butter. Bake in a 180°C (350°F) oven for 40 minutes. Remove quail from pan, remove and discard bacon slices.

3 Replace bacon with vine leaves, tying securely with string. Return quail to roasting pan, baste with brandy. Bake a further 40 minutes. Add broth if the pan gets too dry.

4 Arrange vine-wrapped quail on a heated platter. Spoon over pan juices. Serve hot.

Serves 4

Caraway Roast Chicken

2 tspn caraway seeds

60g (2oz) unsalted butter, room temperature

1 x 1.5kg (3lb) chicken

½ cup chicken stock

1½ tblspn flour

2 tblspn dry white wine

1 Place 2 teaspoons of the caraway seeds in a coffee grinder, pulverise. Beat butter in a small bowl until fluffy, stir in caraway powder. Shape caraway-butter mixture into a small cylinder, wrap in foil, seal securely, refrigerate until stiff, about 2 hours.

2 Carefully loosen skin from chicken breast. Cut caraway butter into thin slices, use about ¾ to slip between skin and breast meat. Melt remaining caraway butter. Reserve.

3 Sprinkle half remaining whole caraway seeds inside chicken cavity. Place chicken breast-side up on a rack in a roasting pan. Brush with half of the reserved melted caraway butter.

4 Roast chicken in a 180°C (350°F) oven for 30 minutes, brush with remaining half of the caraway butter, roast a further 90 minutes, basting with pan juices every 20 minutes. Remove from oven, keep warm.

5 Combine juices from roasting pan and any accumulated juices inside chicken. Skim about 2 tablespoons of fat off the top, place in a frying pan. Discard any remaining fat. To remaining juice add enough water to make 1 cup, reserve.

6 Add flour to fat in frying pan, cook over moderate heat for 2 minutes. Add reserved chicken juices, stock and wine. Cook until sauce starts to thicken. Simmer, stirring constantly, for 3 minutes. Season with salt and freshly ground pepper.

7 Carve chicken into serving pieces. Serve warm with the hot sauce.

Serves 4

Double Chicken Burgers

500g (1lb) chicken mince

1 egg, lightly beaten

½ cup fresh breadcrumbs

2 tspn Worcestershire sauce

3 tblspn butter

4 hamburger buns

1 Combine mince with egg, breadcrumbs and Worcestershire sauce; mix well. Mould mixture into 8 patties.

2 Fry in melted butter until golden, pushing down patties with a spatula, approximately 3 minutes each side. Drain patties on absorbent paper.

3 Place patties in hamburger bun with salad if desired.

Serves 4

Bacardi and Mushroom Chicken Breasts

¼ cup Bacardi rum

30g (1oz) dried mushrooms

1 thick skinned orange

4 skinless chicken breasts

½ cup chicken stock

¼ cup cream

1 Place rum in a small saucepan, heat to nearly boiling. Grate orange skin into rum, cool, stand 3 hours. Soak mushrooms in warm water for 3 hours.

2 Remove any visible fat and sinews from chicken breasts. In a non-stick frying pan, large enough to hold chicken in one layer, brown chicken 7 minutes on one side.

3 Remove mushrooms from soaking liquor, reserve liquor, add mushrooms to chicken. Turn chicken, cook other side about 7 minutes, tossing mushrooms. Remove chicken and mushrooms from pan, keep warm.

Double Chicken Burgers (top); Chicken Strips with Prosciutto and Tomato Sauce

4 Reheat mushroom liquor, strain together with orange-flavoured bacardi into the frying pan, add chicken stock. Reduce over medium high heat until sauce starts to thicken.

5 Add cream, heat through, do not boil again. Season to taste with salt and freshly ground black pepper.

6 Serve chicken breasts on heated plates, pour sauce all around and garnish with mushrooms.

Serves 4

Chicken Strips with Prosciutto and Tomato Sauce

4 chicken breasts fillets

1 cup of plain flour, for coating

4 tblspn butter

¾ cup dry white wine

3 cups tinned peeled tomatoes, with juice

60g (2oz) prosciutto, cut into strips

1 Chop chicken into 3cm (1¼in) strips and coat with flour.

2 Melt the butter in a large frying pan, add chicken and cook for 5 minutes, stirring constantly.

3 Pour in the wine and tomatoes and add prosciutto. Bring mixture to the boil, reduce heat and simmer for 15 minutes.

4 Serve immediately, with rice if desired.

Serves 4

Lime Rum Chicken

1.5kg (3lb) chicken, cut into 4cm (1½in) pieces

3 limes

¾ cup white rum

¼ cup soy sauce

2 garlic cloves, crushed

1 Dry chicken pieces with paper towels. Place in a bowl. Squeeze the juice from 2 limes, pour over chicken in bowl.

2 In a small bowl combine rum, soy sauce and crushed garlic. Pour over chicken, combine well. Cover, refrigerate at least 5 hours, or overnight.

3 Drain chicken, dredge in flour. Deep-fry chicken pieces in batches in hot oil, turning once, until golden, about 5 minutes. Drain on paper towels. Serve hot with wedges of remaining lime.

Serves 4

Quail Pan-fried with Ham

1 tspn thyme

8 quail, split and flattened, giblets removed

½ cup unsalted butter

250g (½lb) ham, cut into matchsticks

1 Season quail with salt, freshly ground pepper and crumbled thyme.

2 In a frying pan melt butter over medium high heat. When foam starts to subside add quail, skin side down. Sprinkle with ham, cover pan, cook until skin is golden, about 3 minutes.

3 Turn quail, cook other side until juices run clear, about 4 minutes. Remove to a heated platter, keep warm.

4 Remove fat from pan, add ¼ cup water. Cook 1 minute over high heat, scraping up any browned bits. Pour over quail, serve hot.

Serves 4

Roasted Chicken with Rosemary and Carrots

Roasted Chicken with Rosemary and Carrots

1 size 18 uncooked chicken

5 sprigs of rosemary

5 carrots, peeled, cut in half lengthwise

3 tblspn redcurrant jelly

2 tblspn melted butter

1 tspn fine white pepper

1 Wash chicken and place 3 of the sprigs of rosemary into cavity. Place chicken in a large baking dish with carrots alongside.

2 In a small saucepan, over medium heat, melt jelly, add butter and pepper. Chop the remaining sprigs of rosemary into small pieces and add to melted jelly mixture.

3 Brush mixture over chicken. Cook chicken and carrots in moderate oven 45 minutes to one hour, basting regularly with jelly mixture, and turning carrots frequently.

Serves 4

Roast Quail with Soy Honey Glaze

2 fresh quail

2 tspn sesame oil

2 tblspn soy sauce

2 tblspn honey

1 tblspn lemon juice

2 tspn sesame seeds

1 Wash quail and tie legs together with string.

Roast Quail with Soy Honey Glaze

2 In medium saucepan, combine sesame oil, soy sauce, honey, lemon juice and sesame seeds. Stir over medium heat for 10 minutes.

3 Brush quail with the soy honey glaze and place in a small baking dish. Bake in moderate oven for 25 minutes, basting regularly with the glaze. Serve with fresh vegetables if desired.

Serves 1

Old-fashioned Chicken

1 x 2kg (4lb) chicken

1 onion

6 carrots

6 potatoes

1 whole head garlic, unpeeled

1 Cut chicken into 8 pieces, slice onion, peel and halve carrots, peel and halve potatoes.

2 Put chicken into a large saucepan with water to cover. Bring to a boil, skim froth off the top.

3 Add onion and salt and freshly ground pepper to taste. Cover, reduce heat to a simmer, cook 30 minutes.

4 Add carrots, potatoes and garlic. Add more water if necessary. Continue simmering a further 30 minutes.

5 Discard garlic. Serve chicken and vegetables in large heated bowls with some broth poured over each portion.

Serves 4

Herbed Chicken in Foil

4 chicken breast halves, skinned and boned

4 tblspn chopped fresh herbs, chives, basil, tarragon (any fresh herb will do)

½ cup freshly squeezed lemon juice

1 small onion, very thinly sliced, rings separated

⅓ cup unsalted butter

1 Place each chicken breast half on a large piece of foil. Sprinkle each with 1 tablespoon herbs, 2 tablespoons lemon juice, a few onions rings, 1 tablespoon butter, salt and freshly ground pepper to taste.

2 Bake in a 190°C (375°F) oven for 30 minutes. Place on heated plates. Open parcels. Serve immediately.

Serves 4

Chicken Pieces with Artichoke Sauce

4 tblspn butter

1 medium uncooked chicken, jointed

¼ cup white wine

1½ cup cream

1 cup chicken stock

1 cup artichoke hearts, drained

1 Melt butter over medium heat in a large frypan. Add chicken pieces and cook for 5 minutes, turning frequently.

2 Remove chicken pieces from pan and place in baking dish, cook in moderate oven for 20 minutes. Add wine, cream and stock to pan juices.

3 Chop half of the artichokes into small pieces and add to wine and cream sauce. Bring mixture to the boil, reduce heat and simmer 10 minutes or until sauce thickens.

4 Strain sauce and return to frying pan. Add baked chicken pieces and remaining whole artichoke hearts to sauce and serve immediately.

Serves 4

Sauteed Chicken with Lemon Zest

4 tblspn butter

2 chicken breast fillets

1 cup chicken stock

1 lemon

3 tblspn honey

1 tblspn Italian parsley, chopped

1 Melt butter over medium heat in medium frying pan. Add chicken fillets and saute 2 minutes each side or until cooked through.

2 Remove fillets from frying pan and add chicken stock to the pan. Bring to boil, reduce heat, simmer 5 minutes.

3 Remove zest from lemon with a sharp knife and cut zest strips into thin shreds. Place shreds in a bowl of iced water and set aside.

Chicken Pieces with Artichoke Sauce (top left); Sauteed Chicken with Lemon Zest (lower left); Smoked Chicken and Melon Salad (above)

4 Juice the remainder of the lemon and add to simmering stock. Add the honey and simmer stock for a further 5 minutes or until reduced to ¼ cup.

5 Add zest and fillets to pan, cook 1 minute. Serve immediately.

Serves 2

Smoked Chicken and Melon Salad

¼ small watermelon

½ honeydew melon

½ rockmelon

1 small smoked chicken

1 small bunch coriander

¼ cup French dressing

1 Remove skin and seeds from melons and cut into batons.

2 Cut chicken away from bones and discard carcass.

3 Chop coriander very roughly and mix with chicken pieces and melon.

4 Arrange salad decoratively on serving plate, pour dressing over top. Decorate with extra coriander and cracked pepper if desired.

Serves 4

Chicken with Mushrooms and Gruyere

4 large half chicken breasts, boned

3 eggs, lightly beaten

1 cup dry breadcrumbs

½ cup butter

500g (1lb) mushrooms, sliced

4 slices Gruyere cheese

1 Place chicken in bowl, pour over beaten eggs. Cover, refrigerate 1 hour. Drain, cover with breadcrumbs, shaking off excess.

2 Melt ⅓ cup butter in a frying pan, cook chicken until golden, about 3 minutes each side. Transfer to an ovenproof dish.

3 Melt remaining butter in the frying pan. Add mushrooms, cook about 5 minutes, until soft. Arrange over chicken pieces.

4 Put cheese slices on top of mushrooms, pour ¼ cup of water into the dish. Bake in a 180°C (350°F) oven about 20 minutes, or until chicken juices run clear when pierced, and cheese is bubbly. Serve hot.

Serves 4

Main Course Salads

The word "salad" takes on a new meaning with these crisp and crunchy main course dishes. They're not only fresh tasting and healthy, they're also satisfying.

Potato, Asparagus, Ham and Gruyere Salad

4 potatoes, peeled, halved

1kg (2lb) asparagus, trimmed, cut into 5cm (2in) pieces

375g (¾lb) ham, cut into strips

185g (6oz) Gruyere cheese, cut into sticks

1 tblspn Dijon mustard

⅓ cup vinaigrette

1 Boil potatoes in lightly salted boiling water until just tender. Drain. Cut into thick slices crosswise.

2 Plunge asparagus into lightly salted boiling water, return to a boil, cook 3 minutes. Drain, rinse under cold running water. Pat dry with paper towels.

3 Combine potatoes, asparagus, ham and Gruyere in a salad bowl. Whisk mustard into vinaigrette.

4 Pour vinaigrette over salad, toss well to coat. Serve at room temperature.

Serves 4

Roast Beef Salad

2 cups minced rare roast beef

1 cup sliced cooked potatoes

1 cup roughly chopped Cos lettuce

1 cup crunchy cooked French beans, halved

1 cup sliced radish

¾ cup egg mayonnaise

1 Combine beef, potatoes, lettuce, beans and radish in a salad bowl. Toss gently.

2 Add mayonnaise, toss again, making sure everything is coated evenly. Cover, refrigerate 1 hour. Serve cold.

Serves 4

Beef and Potato Salad

3 large potatoes, peeled

3 cups beef steak, cooked and cut into strips

2 pimentos, cut into strips

3 tblspn olive oil

¼ cup red wine vinegar

1 lettuce

1 Using a melon-baller, scoop the potatoes into small balls until you have 2 cups.

2 Cook potato balls in salted boiling water until tender, drain.

3 Combine potatoes, beef, pimentos, olive oil and vinegar. Toss well.

4 Serve salad on a bed of lettuce. Garnish with a sprig of parsley and black cracked pepper if desired.

Serves 4-6

Beef and Potato Salad

Spinach and Prawn (Shrimp) Salad with Curry Dressing

Spinach and Prawn (Shrimp) Salad with Curry Dressing

1 bunch spinach, stems removed

1 cup cooked medium prawns (shrimp), shelled, tails intact and deveined

1 avocado, peeled, pitted and sliced

½ cup sour cream

½ cup plain yoghurt

1 tspn curry powder

1 Tear spinach into bite-size pieces and arrange on serving plate with prawns and avocado slices.

2 In a small bowl combine sour cream, yoghurt and curry powder, mix well.

3 Pour dressing over salad and garnish with fresh mint if desired.

Serves 2-3

Marinated Tuna with Coconut

4 fresh tuna steaks, skinned, boned and diced

1 cup fresh lime juice

1 red onion, peeled and chopped finely

2 capsicum (peppers), red and/or green

½ cup coconut cream

¼ cup shredded coconut, toasted

1 In a large bowl, combine tuna with lime juice and marinate for 4 hours in the refrigerator.

2 Remove tuna with a slotted spoon and place in a medium bowl with the onion. Reserve marinade.

3 Seed capsicum and chop roughly. Add capsicum, coconut cream and 3 tablespoons of the reserved marinade to the tuna and onion, mix well.

4 Spoon salad onto serving plates, sprinkle with toasted coconut and garnish with fresh coriander if desired.

Serves 4

Radicchio and Chicken Salad with Spanish Onion Dressing

750g (1½lb) boned, skinned chicken breasts

1 tblspn crumbled fresh thyme

1 small Spanish onion

1 radicchio lettuce

⅓ cup olive oil

¼ cup red wine vinegar

1 Cut chicken into 2.5cm (1in) cubes. Sprinkle with thyme, season to taste with salt and freshly ground pepper.

2 Slice onion very thinly, separate rings. Rinse radicchio, drain, dry, refrigerate.

Crunchy Chicken Salad

3 Heat half of the oil in a frying pan. Add chicken, saute about 5 minutes, until barely cooked through. Remove from pan. Keep warm. Add vinegar to pan, scraping up any browned bits.

4 Remove from heat, add onion and remaining oil. Season to taste with salt and freshly ground pepper.

5 Arrange radicchio on a chilled platter, top with warm chicken and spoon over Spanish onion mixture.

Note: This salad can be served chilled. Reserve chicken and Spanish onion vinaigrette separately, covered, in refrigerator.

Serves 4

Crunchy Chicken Salad

4 chicken breast fillets, cooked, cut into strips

1 cup sour cream

½ cup mayonnaise

1 cup celery, cut into thin strips, 3cm (1¼in) long

½ cup spring onions (scallions), chopped

½ cup pecan nuts, roughly chopped

1 Place chicken in a large bowl.

2 Whisk sour cream and mayonnaise together until smooth and add to chicken.

3 Add celery, spring onions and pecans, toss well. Refrigerate before serving. Garnish with Italian parsley if desired.

Serves 4

Pasta Salad with Snow Peas and Salami

155g (5oz) pasta shells

185g (6oz) snow peas

125g (4oz) sliced Italian salami, cut into matchsticks

1 carrot, cut into matchsticks

½ cup shredded mozzarella cheese

⅓ cup vinaigrette

1 Cook shells in lightly salted boiling water until tender. Drain. Rinse under cold running water. Drain.

2 Plunge snow peas into lightly salted boiling water, return to a boil, cook 30 seconds, drain. Rinse under cold running water, drain. Pat dry with paper towels.

3 In a salad bowl combine pasta shells, snow peas, salami, carrot and mozzarella. Drizzle with vinaigrette. Toss well. Serve cold.

Serves 4

Herring Salad

2 pickled herrings

5 potatoes

2 Granny Smith apples, unpeeled

2 dill pickles

⅓ cup vinaigrette

2 hard-boiled eggs

1 Soak herring in cold water to cover for at least 6 hours, or overnight. Change water every 2 hours. Rinse, dry. Remove skin, cut flesh into 1cm (½in) pieces. Place in a bowl.

2 Boil potatoes in their skin until just tender. Peel, cut into 1cm (½in) pieces. Add to herring.

3 Dice apples into 1cm (½in) pieces, add to herring and potato. Cut dill pickles into 0.5cm (¼in) pieces, add to herring bowl. Toss gently, cover, refrigerate for 2 hours.

4 Toss salad with vinaigrette, arrange on a chilled platter, garnish with hard-boiled egg wedges. Serve chilled.

Serves 4

Butter Bean and Bacon Salad

250g (½lb) broccoli flowerets

200g (6½oz) snow peas

6 rashers bacon

2 cups butter beans, rinsed and drained

1 tspn chopped Italian parsley

¼ cup French dressing

1 Bring a large saucepan of water to the boil, add broccoli and cook for 2 minutes. Remove with a slotted spoon and refresh with cold water.

2 Add snow peas to boiling water, cook 30 seconds, refresh with cold water.

3 Remove rind from bacon and cut into thin strips, 3cm (1¼in). Cook bacon in a medium frypan, stirring constantly until lightly browned.

4 In a large bowl combine broccoli, snow peas, bacon, beans, parsley and dressing, toss well.

Serves 4

Creamy Roasted Duck Salad

1 medium duck

2 tblspn oil

2 red onions, chopped

¾ cup chicken stock

½ cup dry white wine

¾ cup sour cream

1 Season skin of duck with salt and pepper. Bake in a moderate oven for 1 hour or until cooked through. Remove duck from pan and allow to cool.

2 Pour out all the fat from the pan and replace with oil. Add onion and place pan over medium heat. Cook onions for 5 minutes or until tender.

3 Pour in stock and cook for 8 minutes. Add wine, bring to the boil, reduce and simmer for 5 minutes, scraping bottom of pan with a wooden spoon.

4 Pour sauce into a large bowl and cool to room temperature.

5 When duck is cool enough to handle remove meat from bones, cut into large dice and add to sauce.

6 Add the sour cream to sauce and stir until combined. Serve at room temperature or slightly chilled. Garnish with parsley if desired.

Serves 4

*Butter Bean and Bacon Salad (top);
Creamy Roasted Duck Salad*

Lime Marinated Lemon Sole

750g (1½lb) lemon sole fillet

juice of 6 limes

2 tblspn olive oil

1 bunch curly endive

1 Cut sole fillets into thin strips. Place in a bowl, pour over lime juice, cover, refrigerate 3 hours.

2 Toss sole strips with oil, season to taste with salt and freshly ground pepper.

3 Clean endive in several changes of cold water. Separate leaves, arrange on a platter. Spoon sole strips into the centre. Serve cold.

Serves 4

Tuna, Potato and Watercress Salad

2 large bunches watercress

4 potatoes

425g (13½oz) can tuna

1 green capsicum (pepper)

3 tomatoes

⅓ cup vinaigrette

1 Rinse watercress in several changes of cold water, drain, cut into bite-size pieces. Place in a salad bowl.

2 Boil potatoes in their skins until just tender, drain. When cool enough to handle, peel, slice. Cool completely.

3 Drain tuna, divide into 2.5cm (1in) chunks. Seed capsicum, cut into strips. Cut tomatoes into wedges.

4 Add cooled potatoes, tuna, capsicum and tomatoes to salad bowl. If not serving immediately, cover and refrigerate. Just before serving toss gently with vinaigrette.

Serves 4

Caesar Salad with Chicken

1 Cos lettuce

8 diagonal slices of a baguette

4 chicken breasts, halved, bone removed

50g (2oz) can anchovy fillets, drained, roughly chopped

½ cup Parmesan cheese shavings

⅓ cup vinaigrette

1 Rinse lettuce, separate leaves, dry. Tear into bite-size pieces. Place in a salad bowl.

2 Cut bread into 1cm (½in) cubes. Place on a baking tray under a preheated grill, toast, turning, until golden on all sides, about 2 minutes. Set aside.

3 Season chicken with salt and freshly ground pepper. Place on griller tray skin-side down. Grill about 4 minutes, turn, grill skin-side until golden, about a further 4 minutes. Set aside, cool to room temperature.

4 Add half the vinaigrette to the lettuce in the bowl. Toss well. Add anchovies and cheese shavings, toss again.

5 Cut chicken into 1cm (½in) wide strips, arrange in salad bowl. Add remaining dressing, toss thoroughly but gently. Serve immediately.

Serves 4

Kiwifruit and Salmon Salad

250g (½lb) kiwifruit, peeled, sliced

440g (14oz) can pink salmon, drained, cut into chunks

½ small cucumber, very thinly sliced

½ small lettuce, shredded

⅓ cup salad cream

¼ cup slivered almonds

1 Combine kiwifruit, salmon and cucumber in a bowl. Cover, refrigerate 1 hour.

Pickled Octopus Salad

2 Arrange shredded lettuce on a platter, top with kiwifruit, salmon and cucumber. Drizzle with salad cream.

3 Sprinkle with slivered almonds, serve immediately.

Serves 4

Pickled Octopus Salad

12 baby octopus

1½ cups white wine vinegar

¼ cup sugar

3 cucumbers, sliced

1 tspn yellow mustard seeds

2 tblspn chopped fresh dill

1 Remove heads from octopus and cut up tentacles. Combine with vinegar and sugar in a medium saucepan over medium heat.

2 Bring mixture to the boil, add cucumber and cook for 2 minutes. Remove octopus and cucumber with a slotted spoon, cool.

3 Reheat the vinegar mixture and bring to the boil, simmer for 5 minutes. Cool to room temperature and add to octopus and cucumber.

4 Add the mustard seeds and dill and chill until ready to serve.

5 Place octopus and cucumber onto serving plate, pour a little vinegar marinade over the top and garnish with fresh chilli pieces.

Serves 6

Smoked Chicken and Apple Salad with Walnut Vinaigrette

Smoked Chicken and Apple Salad with Walnut Vinaigrette

½ cup chopped walnuts

1 smoked chicken, bones removed

2 apples

¼ cup white wine vinegar

¼ cup walnut oil

1 tblspn finely chopped fresh coriander

1 Bake walnuts, stirring occasionally, in a shallow pan in a moderate oven 25 minutes, or until toasted.

2 Remove skin from chicken and cut chicken in strips.

3 Cut apples in quarters, remove seeds then cut each quarter into 3 slices.

4 In a large bowl combine vinegar, walnut oil and chopped coriander. Add the walnuts, chicken and apples to vinaigrette, toss well.

5 Arrange salad on serving plate, garnish with fresh dill if desired.

Serves 4

Chicken and Apple Coleslaw

4 cups shredded cabbage

1 Granny Smith apple, unpeeled, cut into 1cm (½in) cubes

½ cup coleslaw salad dressing

375g (¾lb) boned, skinned chicken breasts, cooked

1 In a salad bowl combine cabbage, apple and salad dressing.

2 Cut chicken into 1cm (½in) wide strips. Add to bowl, toss gently to coat well. Cover, refrigerate until ready to serve. Serve cold.

Serves 4

RICE AND PASTA

With rice and pasta in your pantry you need never wonder what to cook for dinner. Just try these recipes and wait for the compliments.

Chunky Lentil and Tomato Salad

⅔ cup red lentils, rinsed

2 medium tomatoes, chopped

⅓ cup Italian parsley, chopped

2 tblspn French dressing

3 tblspn olive oil

1 Soak lentils in warm water for 10-15 minutes or until slightly softened.

2 Mix tomatoes and parsley, pour over combined dressing and oil; toss gently.

Serves 4

Golden Coconut Rice

2 cups Basmati rice

½ tspn turmeric

½ tspn cumin

¾ cups coconut milk

1 In a flameproof casserole combine rice, turmeric, cumin and coconut milk. Add half a teaspoon salt and 2½ cups water. Stir well to combine.

2 Bring to a boil, reduce heat to low, cook covered for 15 minutes. Remove from heat, stir briskly with a fork to fluff, cover again, stand a further 10 minutes. Serve hot.

Serves 6

Chunky Lentil and Tomato Salad (top); Gnocchi Alla Romana

Gnocchi Alla Romana

1 cup chicken stock

3 cups milk

6 tblspn butter

1 cup cornmeal

⅔ cup Parmesan cheese

¼ tspn nutmeg

1 In a large saucepan, bring the stock and milk to the boil over a medium heat, add 2 tablespoons of the butter.

2 Mix cornmeal with 1 cup cold water; mix to a smooth paste. Slowly pour cornmeal into milk, stirring vigorously, until cornmeal mixture is smooth and very thick.

3 Line a flat pan with greaseproof paper, pour mixture over it, smoothing the surface with a wet knife; leave to cool completely.

4 Grease the bottom of a baking tray with 1 tablespoon of the butter. Cut out rounds of the cornmeal mixture with a biscuit cutter, about 4cm (1½ in) diameter, and fold each round in half.

5 Place on prepared tray, melt remaining butter and pour over gnocchi. Sprinkle the Parmesan cheese and nutmeg evenly over the whole surface. Cook in moderate oven 20-25 minutes, or until golden.

Serves 6

Neopolitan Pizza

2 rounds of flatbread

4 tblspn tomato paste

2 tblspon white wine

2 cups chopped tomato pulp, seeded

2 cups freshly grated Mozzarella cheese

1 can anchovies

1 Mix tomato paste and wine together, divide mixture in two, spread over each flatbread.

2 Cover with tomatoes and Mozzarella.

3 Arrange anchovies like lattice on top of cheese. Add a sprinkle of herbs if desired, bake in moderate oven 20-30 minutes.

Serves 4

Pearl Barley and Potato Casserole

1kg (2lb) potatoes, unpeeled

155g (5oz) pearl barley

2 tblspn chopped fresh dill

1¾ cups milk

2 tblspn butter, melted

1 Cook potatoes in lightly salted boiling water until just tender. When cool enough to handle, peel and cut into 0.5cm (¼in) slices.

2 Rinse barley thoroughly under cold running water, drain. Place in a saucepan with water to cover, add a pinch of salt, bring to a boil. Reduce heat, simmer 10 minutes, drain.

3 Grease an ovenproof serving dish. Make a layer of half the potatoes, season with salt and freshly ground pepper. Cover with all the barley, sprinkle with dill.

4 Top with remaining potato slices, season with salt and freshly ground pepper. Pour in milk, brush top potato layer generously with butter.

5 Bake in a 180°C (350°F) oven for 1 hour or until potatoes are golden. Serve hot.

Serves 4

Neopolitan Pizza

Pasta Shells with Prawn (Shrimp) and Tomato Sauce

¾ cup olive oil

2 cloves garlic, halved

3 x 425g (13½oz) cans Italian peeled tomatoes, drained

2 tblspn finely chopped continental parsley

250g (½lb) uncooked prawns (shrimp)

500g (1lb) pasta shells

1 Combine oil and garlic in a heavy saucepan, cook over moderate heat until garlic is brown. Discard garlic.

2 Halve tomatoes, squeeze gently to remove seeds, add to hot oil. Simmer about 8 minutes, breaking up tomatoes with a wooden spoon. The sauce should stay lumpy. Add parsley, season to taste with salt and freshly ground pepper.

3 Rinse prawns under cold running water, pat dry with paper towels. Cut in half. Add to hot tomato sauce, stir over heat until prawns change colour, about 3 minutes. Correct seasoning. Keep warm.

4 Meanwhile cook pasta shells in salted boiling water until tender. Drain. Place in a heated bowl. Pour sauce over shells, toss to coat well. Serve immediately.

Serves 4

Spaghetti with Raw Tomatoes and Herbs

750g (1½lb) ripe tomatoes

½ cup chopped mixed fresh herbs, make sure the mixture includes basil

500g (1lb) spaghetti, preferably fresh

½ cup olive oil

Creamy Barley Casserole

6 corn cobs, kernels removed

1 cup chopped bacon

1 cup barley

1 tspn ground cumin

3 cups thickened cream

1 cup sliced pimentos, sliced

1 Fry bacon over low heat, stirring constantly until crispy.

2 Boil 5 cups water with salt, add barley, cook 30 minutes, skimming surface occasionally. Rinse under cold water, drain.

3 Place corn, bacon, cumin and cream into large saucepan, boil until reduced by ⅓; add to barley mixture, stir in pimentos.

4 Transfer mixture to a casserole and cover. Bake in a preheated oven, 180°C (350°F) until heated through, about 25 minutes. Serve immediately.

Serves 6

Fettucine with Radicchio and Goat Cheese

2 cups cream

1 clove garlic, crushed

500g (1lb) fettucine

125g (4oz) goat cheese, crumbled

1 cup tightly packed radicchio leaves, rinsed, cut into strips

1 Combine cream and garlic in a saucepan, bring to a boil. Cook over moderate heat until cream is slightly reduced, about 6 minutes.

2 Bring a large pot of salted water to a boil, add fettucine, cook until al dente, drain.

3 Add goat cheese to cream, stir over low heat until cheese is melted.

4 Place fettucine into a heated bowl, add cream sauce and radicchio, season to taste with salt and freshly ground pepper. Toss to mix well. Serve immediately.

Serves 4

Continental Bean Casserole (top); Creamy Barley Casserole

1 Wipe tomatoes with a damp cloth, halve, squeeze to remove seeds, cut into 1cm (½in) cubes. Combine with chopped herbs in a pasta bowl.

2 Bring a large pot of salted water to a boil, add spaghetti, cook until pasta is tender, but not too soft. Drain.

3 Meanwhile, heat olive oil over high heat to smoking. Immediately pour oil over tomatoes and herb in the bowl. Season with salt and freshly ground black pepper. Mix well.

4 Add hot pasta to bowl, toss thoroughly with tomato and herb mixture. Serve immediately.

Serves 4

Continental Bean Casserole

5 rashers bacon, chopped

1 large onion, chopped

2 tinned tomatoes

3 cups mixed beans, drained and rinsed

2 capsicum (pepper), seeded and chopped

500g (1lb) continental frankfurts, cooked and drained.

1 Place bacon and onion in a large saucepan, cook over low heat 5 minutes, stirring constantly.

2 Add tomatoes, beans and capsicum plus 2 cups of water. Slowly bring to the boil, reduce heat and simmer 20 minutes.

3 Cut frankfurts into large chunks and add to casserole, cook further 10 minutes.

Serves 6

Tomato and Chive Pilaf

60g (2oz) unsalted butter

375g (12oz) long-grain rice

500g (1lb) tomatoes, peeled, coarsely chopped

2 tblspn chopped fresh chives

600ml (1 pint) boiling chicken stock

1 Melt butter in a heavy saucepan. Add rice, saute 3 minutes. Add tomatoes, chives and stock. Season to taste with salt and freshly ground pepper. Stir well to combine.

2 Bring to a boil, cover, reduce heat to a simmer, cook about 18 minutes or until rice is tender and all the liquid has been absorbed.

3 Remove from heat, set aside for 10 minutes. Stir briskly with a fork. Serve as a side dish for roast meats or grilled or oven-baked fish.

Serves 6

Spaghetti in Cream Sauce with Caviar

⅓ cup unsalted butter

1 small onion, finely chopped

2 cups cream

500g (1lb) spaghetti

¼ cup finely chopped fresh continental parsley

50g (2oz) jar caviar

1 Melt butter in a large heavy saucepan. Add onion, saute over medium heat until golden, about 3 minutes. Add cream, bring to a boil. Boil about 8 minutes until sauce thickens. Keep warm.

2 Cook spaghetti in lightly salted boiling water until al dente. Drain. Add to cream sauce, heat through, stirring to coat. Season to taste with salt and freshly ground pepper.

3 Serve spaghetti onto heated plates. Sprinkle with parsley and caviar. Serve immediately.

Serves 4

Pasta with Spinach Sauce

350g (11oz) fresh fettucine

3 tblspn butter

2 cloves garlic, crushed

1 cup cooked spinach, chopped

1½ cups thickened cream

1 cup freshly grated Parmesan cheese

1 In a small pan, melt butter; add garlic and cook 2 minutes.

2 Add cream and cheese, stir until smooth.

3 Transfer mixture into a medium saucepan, stir over low heat.

4 Bring a large saucepan of water to the boil, add fettucine and cook until tender about 7 minutes, strain.

5 Add spinach to saucepan of cream mixture; coat well, serve immediately.

Serves 4

Macaroni with Sun-dried Tomatoes and Prosciutto

3 cups dried macaroni

3 tblspn butter

2 cloves garlic, crushed

¾ cup thinly sliced prosciutto

½ cup sun-dried tomatoes, drained, sliced

½ cup fresh basil, chopped

1 Melt butter in a large saucepan over medium heat. Add garlic and prosciutto, cook 5 minutes then add tomatoes and basil, cook further 2 minutes.

2 Bring a large saucepan of water to the boil; add macaroni and cook until al dente, about 6 minutes.

3 Strain macaroni and mix into prosciutto and tomato mixture. Serve immediately and garnish as desired.

Serves 4

Pasta with Spinach Sauce (top); Macaroni with Sun-dried Tomatoes and Prosciutto. Risotto with Asparagus (right)

Risotto with Asparagus

1 bunch asparagus

2 tblspn butter

2½ cups rice

6 thin slices of prosciutto, finely chopped

6 cups chicken stock, boiling

½ cup fresh grated Parmesan cheese

1 Cut tough part of asparagus from stalks, leaving tender upper stalks and tips. Cut stalks into thin slices.

2 Melt butter in a large saucepan, add rice, asparagus, prosciutto and boiling stock. Cook rice for about 20 minutes or until tender.

3 Remove from heat, stir in cheese.

4 Line 6 timbale tins with greaseproof paper, firmly press risotto mixture into tins, bake in moderate oven 10 minutes.

5 Run a knife around inside edge of tins to loosen; turn out onto serving plate, garnish with salad if desired.

Serves 6

Fettucine with Lemon

¼ cup unsalted butter

1 cup cream

1 tblspn freshly grated lemon zest

500g (1lb) fettucine

½ cup freshly grated Parmesan cheese

1 Melt butter in a saucepan over gentle heat, don't brown. Add cream and lemon zest, stir over heat until the mixture turns a creamy yellow.

2 Cook fettucine in boiling salted water until al dente, drain. Place in a heated bowl, add cream mixture. Toss to combine well. Season to taste with salt and freshly ground pepper.

3 Serve immediately, pass Parmesan cheese separately.

Serves 4

Rigatoni with Sausage and Ricotta Cheese

500g (1lb) Italian sausage (see note)

375g (¾lb) ricotta cheese

½ tspn chilli flakes

½ cup freshly grated Pecorino cheese (see note)

500g (1lb) rigatoni, cooked

1 Remove sausage meat from skin, crumble. Combine with 1 cup water in a saucepan, cover, cook over moderate heat until meat is cooked through, about 10 minutes. Drain, reserve liquid.

2 Place ricotta in a heated bowl, add liquid, stir to make a smooth sauce. Add hot meat and chilli flakes. Add Pecorino cheese, toss well. Correct seasoning. Serve over cooked rigatoni immediately.

Note: Italian sausage and Pecorino cheese are available from Italian delicatessens.

Serves 4

Elbow Macaroni with Blue-veined Cheese

1 cup cream

185g (6oz) blue-veined cheese, cut into cubes

500g (1lb) elbow macaroni

⅓ cup freshly grated Parmesan cheese

1 Combine cream and cheese in a saucepan. Bring to a boil over moderate heat, stirring constantly. Allow to boil for 30 seconds only, remove from heat, set aside.

2 Cook macaroni in a large pot of lightly salted water until tender, drain. Place in a heated bowl.

3 Reheat sauce gently if necessary, pour over pasta, add Parmesan cheese. Toss thoroughly to coat. Season with freshly ground black pepper. Serve immediately.

Serves 4

VEGETABLE ACCOMPANIMENTS

These tasty and attractive side dishes are the perfect partners for both meat and fish main courses.

Carrot and Zucchini (Courgette) Ribbons with Pasta

2 large carrots, peeled

4 zucchini (courgette)

8 thin slices prosciutto, cut into thin strips

2½ cups cream

2 cups cooked pasta

½ cup fresh Parmesan cheese, grated

1 Using a swivel-bladed vegetable peeler, peel a few lengthwise strips from two sides of each carrot and zucchini to create a flat surface. Continue to peel thin strips, discard inner cores.

2 Bring a medium saucepan of water to the boil, add carrot and zucchini strips and blanch 1 minute. Remove carrot and zucchini from water, run cold water over them; drain and set aside.

3 In a large saucepan, bring cream to the boil and reduce by a third. Remove from heat, stir in blanched vegetables, prosciutto, pasta and cheese.

Serves 6

Broadbeans with Bacon

¼ cup olive oil

½ cup chopped onion

250g (½lb) bacon, chopped

2 cups freshly shelled broadbeans, or frozen broadbeans, defrosted

1 Heat olive oil in a heavy saucepan, add onion, saute until golden. Add bacon, saute until brown.

2 Add broadbeans, season with a little salt and freshly ground pepper to taste. Add water to cover. Bring to a boil, reduce heat, simmer for 20 minutes, or until beans are tender. Serve hot.

Serves 4

Chilli Onion Rings

½ cup buttermilk

2 chillies, chopped

2 large onions, peeled cut into ½cm (¼in) rings

2 cups plain flour

2 tblspn chilli sauce or chutney

oil for deep frying

1 Blend or process buttermilk and chillies for 30 seconds. Pour mixture into a medium bowl, add onion rings and toss, coating well with buttermilk mixture.

2 Sift flour into a bowl. Using a slotted spoon, transfer onions to the flour. Thoroughly dredge onions in the flour.

3 Heat oil in a deep saucepan and fry onions until golden brown. Keep onions warm in oven at 150°C (300°F). Serve onions with a chilli sauce or chutney.

Serves 4

Carrot and Zucchini (Courgette) Ribbons with Pasta (top); Chilli Onion Rings

Turnip and Kiwifruit Salad

Apple and Onion Puree with Calvados

This puree is a fine accompaniment for pork or game dishes.

3 Granny Smith apples, quartered, cored
1 large onion, peeled, sliced
1 cup dry white wine
½ cup Calvados (see note)
¼ cup unsalted butter
½ cup cream

1 Combine apples, onion, wine, half the Calvados and 2 tablespoons of the butter in a casserole. Simmer over moderate heat, covered, until apples are starting to fall apart and onions are soft, about 35 minutes. Puree mixture in a food processor.

2 Combine mixture with cream in a saucepan, bring to a boil over moderately high heat, cook until thickened, about 8 minutes. Sieve puree, return to the saucepan, add remaining Calvados, return to a boil.

3 Remove from heat, whisk in remaining tablespoon butter. Season to taste with salt and freshly ground pepper. Serve hot.

Note: Calvados is a French apple brandy. If not available substitute with plain brandy.

Serves 4

Turnip and Kiwifruit Salad

4 kiwifruits, peeled and sliced
3 turnips, peeled and sliced
1 chicken stock cube, crumbled
cracked black pepper
¼ cup oil
4 tblspn lime juice

1 Bring a large pan of water to the boil, add stock and turnips, cook for 3 minutes, strain.

2 Arrange slices of kiwifruit and turnips decoratively on a serving plate.

3 Dress with combined pepper, oil and lime juice.

Serves 4

Potato with Capsicum (Pepper) and Prosciutto Bake

4 large potatoes, peeled, cut into 1cm (½in) slices
2 Spanish onions, each cut into 8 wedges
4 red capsicum (peppers), seeded, cut into thick strips
125g (4oz) medium thick sliced prosciutto, cut into julienne
1 tspn chopped fresh rosemary
¼ cup olive oil

1 Combine potato, onion, capsicum, prosciutto and rosemary in a large bowl. Add salt and freshly ground pepper to taste, drizzle with oil. Combine all ingredients thoroughly, this is best done with your hands.

Golden Nugget and Snow Pea Salad with Dill Dressing

2 Place in a large ovenproof serving dish. Bake in a 200°C (400°F) oven for at least 1 hour, stirring every 15 minutes, until potato is golden and crispy. Serve hot.

Serves 6

Tomatoes Stuffed with Olives

1 cup fresh coarse breadcrumbs
1/3 cup coarsely chopped black olives
2 tblspn freshly grated Parmesan cheese
1 clove garlic, crushed
2 tblspn olive oil
4 medium tomatoes

1 In a bowl combine bread-crumbs, olives, Parmesan cheese and garlic. Season with freshly ground black pepper. Add oil, mix well.

2 Cut a very thin slice off the bottom of tomatoes, so they don't topple. Cut off top quarter, reserve top. Hollow out tomato.

3 Divide filling mixture among tomatoes, place tomatoes in an ovenproof serving dish. Place tomato tops alongside tomatoes, cut side up.

4 Place dish in a 250°C (500°F) oven on the highest rack. Bake for 5 minutes or until filling is crispy on top. Replace tops, serve hot.

Serves 4

Golden Nugget and Snow Pea Salad with Dill Dressing

1 Golden nugget pumpkin, seeded
220g (7oz) snow peas
220g (7oz) baby squash, sliced
1 tblspn chopped fresh dill
2 tblspn lemon juice
1/4 cup olive oil

1 Bring a large saucepan of water to a boil. Cut pumpkin into wedges, about 2cm (3/4in) thick, cook in boiling water for 3 minutes.

2 Remove with a slotted spoon, refresh under cold water, drain. Add snow peas and squash to boiling water, cook for 1 minute. Remove with a slotted spoon, refresh under cold water, drain.

3 Place vegetables in a serving dish and toss in combined dill, lemon juice and oil. Serve at room temperature or chilled.

Serves 4

Tasty Roast Potatoes with Bacon

4 large potatos, peeled

¼ cup oil

1 tblspn hazelnut oil

6 rashers bacon

¼ tspn white pepper

¼ tspn nutmeg

1 Cut potatoes into quarters and blanch in a large saucepan of boiling water for 5 minutes, drain.

2 Place potatoes in a baking dish, add the oil, hazelnut oil and sprinkle with 2 teaspoons of salt, mix well.

3 Bake potatoes in moderate oven for 30 minutes, turning occasionally.

4 Remove rind from bacon and chop into small pieces. Sprinkle bacon, pepper and nutmeg over potatoes, cook a further 10 minutes.

Serves 4-6

Creamed Shredded Lettuce with Mimosa Topping

⅓ cup unsalted butter

1 large onion, chopped

8 cups loosely packed lettuce leaves, rinsed, dried, coarsely shredded

1 cup cream

1 tblspn lemon juice

2 hard-boiled eggs, mashed with a fork

1 Melt half of the butter in a large heavy frying pan, add onion, saute until golden. Add lettuce and remaining butter. Cook over medium heat for 5 minutes, stirring from time to time.

2 Add cream and lemon juice. Season to taste with salt and freshly ground pepper. Cook over medium high heat until liquid has evaporated.

3 Serve creamed lettuce on heated plates, sprinkled with mashed hard-boiled egg.

Serves 4

Sauteed Shredded Beets with Walnuts

¼ cup walnuts

2 large beets

⅓ cup unsalted butter

1 Place walnuts on a baking sheet, bake in a 180°C (350°F) oven until starting to colour. Cool, chop.

2 Peel beets, shred in a food processor.

3 Melt butter in a heavy frying pan. Add beet and saute over medium-high heat until starting to soften, about 3 minutes. Season to taste with salt and freshly ground pepper.

4 Place beets onto heated plates, serve hot, sprinkled with walnuts.

Serves 4

Ricotta and Hazelnut Stuffed Potatoes

4 large potatoes, washed

½ cup ricotta cheese

2 tblspn fresh Parmesan cheese, grated

¼ cup tinned asparagus, drained and chopped

1 tblspn chopped chives

2 tblspn chopped hazelnuts

1 Boil potatoes until just tender, drain. Cut the tops off and discard. Carefully scoop out the potato, leaving ½cm (¼in) edge intact around the top of potato.

2 In a small bowl mix together potato, ricotta cheese, Parmesan cheese, asparagus and chives.

3 Fill each potato with mixture and top with the hazelnuts. Bake potatoes in a moderate oven for 20-25 minutes.

Serves 4

Tasty Roast Potatoes with Bacon (top); Ricotta and Hazelnut Stuffed Potatoes

Gingered Potato Pancakes

3 large potatoes

3 eggs, lightly beaten

1 tblspn grated fresh ginger

about ¾ cup peanut oil

1 Peel potatoes, grate coarsely. Place in a sieve, press firmly with hand to extract as much moisture as possible.

2 Transfer to a bowl. Mix in eggs and ginger. Season to taste with salt and freshly ground black pepper. Stir to combine.

3 Heat about 0.5cm (¼in) oil in a large frying pan. Drop heaped tablespoons of the potato mixture into the hot oil, flatten with back of spoon into a 8cm (3in) pancake.

4 Fry over moderately high heat until browned on one side, about 5 minutes, turn over, brown other side, about 4 minutes. Remove to paper towel-lined platter, keep warm in oven until all pancakes are cooked. Serve hot.

Serves 4

Thai Cucumber

¼ cup rice wine vinegar (see note)

1 tspn sugar

1 tblspn grated lemon zest

2 small cucumbers

⅓ cup chopped fresh coriander

1 Combine vinegar, sugar and lemon zest in a small bowl. Add salt to taste and 2 tablespoons water. Stir well to combine.

2 Peel and seed cucumbers. Slice very thinly. Toss cucumbers with dressing. Cover and refrigerate for at least 2 hours.

3 When ready to serve toss with fresh coriander.

Note: Rice wine vinegar is available in Oriental foodstores.

Serves 4

Broccoli with Chilli Hollandaise

500g (1lb) broccoli

6 eggs yolks

½ tspn chilli powder

¼ tspn white pepper

2 tblspn white wine vinegar

¾ cup melted butter, at boiling point

1 Remove stems from broccoli, cut into flowerets. Bring a large saucepan of water to the boil, add broccoli and blanch for 1 minute; drain and refresh with cold water; drain well.

2 Combine egg yolks with chilli powder, pepper and vinegar in a blender, while motor is running pour bubbling hot butter into blender, blend for 1 minute or until mixture thickens. Serve with broccoli.

Serves 4

Spinach with Prosciutto, Raisins and Pinenuts

1kg (2lb) spinach

2 tblspn olive oil

1 clove garlic, finely chopped

5 slices medium thin sliced prosciutto, cut into strips

2 tblspn raisins

2 tblspn pinenuts

1 Rinse spinach in several changes cold water. Place in a saucepan with only the water adhering to it. Add a little salt. Bring to a boil, cook until just tender. Drain. Squeeze to remove all water.

2 Place oil in a frying pan, add garlic and prosciutto, saute until garlic turns golden. Add spinach, toss for 3 minutes to heat through.

3 Add raisins and pinenuts, cook a further 2 minutes to heat through. Season to taste with salt and freshly ground pepper. Serve hot.

Serves 4

Broccoli with Chilli Hollandaise (top); Honey Lemon Glazed Carrots

Mushrooms with Port Glaze

500g (1lb) button mushrooms

¼ cup olive oil

2 tblspn port wine

2 tblspn red wine vinegar

1½ tspn honey

1 Remove mushroom stems, discard or reserve for another use, eg broth. Wipe mushroom caps with a damp cloth.

2 Combine oil, port, vinegar and honey in a frying pan. Add about half a teaspoon salt. Cook over high heat until sizzling.

3 Reduce heat to moderately high, add mushrooms, rounded side down. Cook until mushrooms are a rich red and liquid has reduced to a syrup, about 15 minutes.

4 Turn mushrooms over, cook over high heat 1 minute. Season to taste with salt and freshly ground pepper. Serve hot.

Serves 4

Honey Lemon Glazed Carrots

8 medium carrots, peeled

2 tblspn brown sugar

1 tblspn honey

1 tblspn oil

3 tblspn fresh lime juice

1 tspn butter

1 Cut carrots into batons approximately ½cm x 4cm (¼ x 1½in), and blanch in a saucepan of boiling water for 1 minute, drain.

Poached Baby Beets with Dill Sauce

Fennel with Ham

4 fennel bulbs

¼ cup butter

1 onion, chopped

¾ cup chopped ham

2 cups chicken broth

½ cup grated Parmesan cheese

1 Trim fennel, cut into wedges.

2 Melt butter in a large frying pan. Add onion, saute until golden, about 5 minutes. Add ham and fennel, cook over low heat for 10 minutes, stirring from time to time.

3 Add broth, turn heat up to high, cook until broth has evaporated. Season to taste with salt and freshly ground pepper.

4 Sprinkle with Parmesan cheese, toss quickly, remove from heat. Serve hot.

Serves 4

Oven-baked Kumera (Sweet Potato) Chips

500g (1lb) Kumera (Sweet Potato), peeled

1 tspn sugar

2 tspn freshly squeezed lemon juice

2 tblspn unsalted butter, melted

2 tblspn julienned lemon zest

1 Slice kumera as thinly as possible, rinse in cold water, drain. Pat dry thoroughly with paper towels. Place in a bowl, add sugar, lemon juice and butter. Season to taste with salt and freshly ground pepper.

2 Layer potatoes in a large ovenproof serving dish. Add any liquid remaining in bowl. Cover securely with foil. Bake in a 120°C (250°F) oven for about 50 minutes, or until tender. Serve hot, sprinkled with lemon julienne.

Serves 4

2 In a small saucepan heat the oil and butter. Add sugar, honey, lime juice and ¼ cup water, bring to boil.

3 Reduce heat and cook for 3 minutes or until glaze thickens slightly. Add carrots to glaze and toss.

Serves 4

Poached Baby Beets with Dill Sauce

a bunch of baby beetroot, with stems

½ cup sour cream

½ cup cream

¼ tspn potato flour

2 tblspn dry white wine

1 tblspn chopped dill

1 Wash beetroot and twist off the leaves, leaving a little tuft of stem. Bring a large saucepan of water to the boil, add beetroot and cook for 20 minutes or until just tender.

2 Refresh under cold water and peel. Cut each beetroot in half and drain on absorbent paper.

3 In a medium saucepan combine sour cream, cream, potato flour, and wine. Slowly bring to the boil, stirring constantly until sauce thickens.

4 Remove from heat and stir in the dill. Serve over beetroot, garnished with dill sprig.

Serves 4

DREAMY DESSERTS

*You don't have to have a sweet tooth to enjoy these desserts —
they're simply irresistible.*

Almond Meringue Cream Filled Cookies

¾ cup sugar

4 egg whites

¾ cup ground almonds

½ tspn cream of tartar

25 blanched almond halves

1 cup cream

1 In a medium bowl, and using electric mixer, beat egg whites with sugar until soft peaks form. Fold in ground almonds and cream of tartar.

2 Cover 2 baking trays with greaseproof paper. Drop teaspoonfuls of the mixture, 4cm (1½in) apart on baking trays, smooth the tops and place an almond half on top of biscuit.

3 Bake in moderately slow oven for 20 minutes. Remove from oven and leave to cool on trays for 3 minutes before using a spatula to slide biscuits onto a rack to cool.

4 Continue to cook biscuits as above, making 25 biscuit tops with the almond half on top, and 25 plain biscuits for the bases.

5 Whip cream until thick and pipe a circle of cream on top of each base. Top with almond topped biscuits.

Makes 25

Almond Meringue Cream Filled Cookies

Lemon Mousse with Blueberry Coulis

6 eggs

½ cup sugar

¼ cup lemon juice

1 tblspn gelatine, dissolved in ¼ cup water

1 cup cream, whipped

1 cup tinned blueberries, drained

1 Place 3 of the eggs in a small mixing bowl. Separate the remaining 3 eggs and discard the whites. Place yolks into mixing bowl with the other eggs.

2 Add sugar and beat until mixture is thick and foamy. Pour in lemon juice.

3 Transfer mixture into a large saucepan. Slowly heat mixture, stirring constantly, do not boil. Stir mixture for 20 minutes or until it thickens. Remove from heat.

4 Dissolve gelatine over hot water but do not boil. Pour gelatine into mousse mixture, stirring vigorously.

5 Fold in whipped cream and pour into 4 oiled ramekin dishes. Refrigerate until set.

6 To make coulis; push blueberries through a fine sieve, and chill.

7 To serve, ease mousse away from dish with a knife, pour blueberry coulis over the top of mousse. Serve with fresh fruit if desired.

Serves 4

Grand Marnier Chocolate Mousse

125g (4oz) dark chocolate, cut into 1cm (½in) cubes

3 eggs, separated

2 tblspn Grand Marnier

1 cup cream

¼ cup sugar

whipped cream for garnish (optional)

1 Melt chocolate in the top of a double boiler over simmering water.

2 Place egg yolks in a heavy saucepan, add 1½ tablespoons water. Whisk over *very low* heat until yolks thicken. Add Grand Marnier, continue whisking until sauce coats back of a spoon thickly. Remove from heat.

3 Fold in melted chocolate, transfer mixture to a large bowl.

4 Beat cream until stiff peaks form, when nearly done add 1 tablespoon of the sugar. Fold into the chocolate mixture.

5 Beat egg whites until soft peaks form, add remaining sugar, beat until stiff peaks form. Fold into chocolate mixture.

6 Spoon mixture into a serving dish, cover, refrigerate at least 4 hours, or overnight. Serve garnished with whipped cream if required.

Serves 6

Flambe Strawberries with Vanilla Ice Cream

½ cup sugar

1 slice of lemon

1 tblspn cornflour

4 cups strawberries, washed and hulled

1 glass kirsch, heated

vanilla ice cream

1 Combine sugar and lemon slice in a saucepan with 1½ cups water, bring to a boil. Continue boiling 5 minutes.

2 Add cornflour mixed with a little cold water, cook syrup until slightly thickened.

3 Add strawberries, allow syrup to return to the boil, turn strawberries and syrup into a heatproof serving dish at once.

4 Just before serving, preferably at the table, pour over heated kirsch, ignite. Serve flaming as an accompaniment for ice cream.

Serves 8

Spicy Apple Charlotte

90g (3oz) butter, melted

4 cups unsweetened pie apples

½ cup apricot jam

2 tblspn sultanas

1 tspn ground mixed spice

12 slices white bread (approximately)

1 Heat 3 tablespoons of the butter in a large saucepan. Add pie apples, apricots jam, sultanas and spice, mix well; cook 5 minutes, drain and set side to cool.

2 Remove crusts from bread and cut 5 slices into 3 triangles per slice to fit the bottom of a standard charlotte mould.

3 Dip triangles into remaining butter, and carefully fit them into the bottom of the mould.

4 Cut the remaining bread slices into 2cm (¾in) thick strips. Dip strips in butter and arrange around the sides of mould in upright position over lapping slightly.

5 Fill the mould with the apple mixture and bake in a hot oven for 15 minutes. Reduce heat to 180°C (350°F) and bake for a further 35-40 minutes.

6 Leave charlotte to cool in tin 15 minutes before turning out onto serving plate.

Serves 6

Spicy Apple Charlotte (top); Fresh Peach Pie

Fresh Peach Pie

1 cup plain flour, sifted plus 4 tblspn extra

¾ cup cornflour

225g (7oz) butter, chopped plus 2 tblspn extra

1 egg yolk

3 large peaches, peeled, seeded and sliced

2 tblspn sugar

1 Sift flour and cornflour into a large bowl. Rub in butter until mixture resembles fine breadcrumbs. Add egg yolk and enough water to bind mixture into a dough.

2 Wrap dough in a tea towel and refrigerate 30 minutes. Remove dough from refrigerator and knead for 1 minute.

3 Roll out dough to fit a 23cm oven-proof flan dish, trim edges. Bake blind for 10 minutes in a hot oven.

4 Arrange peach slices in pastry case. Combine extra flour with sugar and sprinkle over peaches.

5 Cut extra butter into small cubes and sprinkle over top of pie. Bake in moderate oven 30-35 minutes.

Serves 6

Brown Sugar and Rum Glazed Grapefruit

2 grapefruit

⅓ cup dark brown sugar

2 tblspn Bundaberg or Jamaica rum

1 Halve grapefruit, seed and cut sections loose from the skin.

2 Sprinkle each half with 1 tablespoon sugar and 2 teaspoons rum.

3 Place under a heated grill, cook until sugar is melted and bubbly, about 3 minutes.

Serves 4

Fresh Orange Jelly

6 oranges

1 lemon

⅓ cup Marsala wine

15g (½oz) leaf gelatine

60g (2oz) sugar

cream (optional)

1 Peel 2 oranges, segment, set aside, discard skin.

2 Wash remaining oranges and lemon, peel the zest, soak zest in Marsala for 1 hour.

3 Combine gelatine and sugar in a bowl, add 150ml (¼ pint) boiling water, stir until gelatine and sugar are dissolved.

4 Strain in Marsala, discard zest. Squeeze the juice from oranges and lemon, add to bowl without straining.

5 Pour into a mould which has been rinsed with cold water, refrigerate until set or overnight.

6 When ready to serve, unmould, serve portions with orange segments and cream if desired.

Serves 4

Coffee Ice Cream with Walnuts and Lychees

125g (4oz) shelled walnuts

good quality store-bought coffee ice cream

½ cup honey, pouring consistency

375g (¾lb) freshly peeled lychees

¼ cup Bundaberg or Jamaica rum (optional)

1 Place walnuts on a baking sheet, toast in a 180°C (350°F) oven until golden, about 10 minutes. Cool.

2 Place scoops of coffee ice cream into 6 individual serving dishes. Drizzle with honey, add a few lychees and sprinkle with walnuts, and rum if desired. Serve at once.

Serves 6

Choc-Coffee Cream Pots

6 eggs yolks

½ cup brown sugar

1½ cups cream

½ cup milk

2 tblspn instant coffee

2 tblspn cocoa

1 In a small bowl, and using an electric mixer, mix egg yolks with ¼ cup of sugar for 1 minute.

2 In a small saucepan, add the cream, milk and remaining sugar, and slowly bring to the boil over a low heat, stirring constantly.

3 Combine coffee and cocoa in a small jug with ¼ cup hot water, mix until smooth.

4 Remove cream mixture from heat and whisk in coffee and cocoa mixture until dissolved. Gradually whisk the custard mixture into the egg yolks until well combined.

5 Gently pour the custard mixture into 6 small ramekins. Place in a deep baking dish and pour 4cm (1½in) of warm water into dish.

6 Cover dish with foil, bake in moderate oven 35 minutes. Remove dishes from water bath and let them cool, refrigerate before serving. Decorate with raspberries if desired.

Makes 6-8

Lemon Pancakes

2 lemons

125g (4oz) flour

60g (2oz) castor sugar

300ml (½ pint) milk

1 egg

2 tblspn butter, melted

1 Grate zest of both lemons, then juice them.

2 Sift flour and sugar into a bowl, add lemon zest.

3 Combine lemon juice with milk and egg, beat well to mix. Slowly pour into flour mixture, stirring constantly. Stir 1 tablespoon of the melted butter into the batter.

4 Heat a frying pan over medium high heat, brush with a little butter, pour in enough batter to just coat base of pan. When golden on one side, turn over, cook other side. Keep warm until all pancakes have been cooked.

5 Serve hot with a mixture of fresh berries, if desired.

Makes about 8 pancakes

Golden Nugget Souffle with Maple Cream

1kg (2lb) Golden Nugget pumpkin

4 eggs

¼ cup maple syrup

1 cup cream

¼ cup brown sugar

1 tspn vanilla essence

1 Boil Golden Nugget until tender. Discard seeds, scoop out flesh, puree.

2 Separate eggs. Beat egg yolks in a large bowl until pale and thick. Add 1 cup pureed pumpkin, 2 tablespoon of the maple syrup, half a cup cream, brown sugar, vanilla and about ¼ teaspoon salt. Mix well.

3 In another bowl beat egg whites until stiff peaks form, fold into pumpkin mixture. Spoon mixture into a buttered 4-cup souffle dish. Bake in a 180°C (350°F) oven until puffed and golden, about 40 minutes.

4 Meanwhile whip remaining ½ cup cream with remaining tablespoon maple syrup until stiff peaks form.

5 Serve souffle immediately it comes out of the oven with maple flavoured cream.

Serves 4

Choc-Coffee Cream Pots

Mango Mousse with Raspberry Coulis

Raspberry Custard with Brown Rice

⅓ cup brown rice

3 large egg yolks

¼ cup sugar

1½ cup cream

1 tspn vanilla essence

1½ cup raspberries

1 Cook rice in very lightly salted boiling water until tender, about 30 minutes, drain.

2 Blend yolks in a large bowl with sugar, cream and vanilla.

3 Divide raspberries among 4 custard cups, spoon rice over berries. Top with cream mixture. Very gently stir to combine ingredients.

4 Place cups in a baking pan, pour in hot water to come up halfway up the side of the cups. Bake in a 180°C (350°F) oven until firm, about 45 minutes.

5 Remove pan from oven, allow to cool until water is tepid. Remove cups, refrigerate at least 2 hours or overnight. Serve cold.

Serves 4

Mango Mousse with Raspberry Coulis

1½ cups thickened cream

¾ cup tinned mangoes

2 tblspn icing sugar

15g (½oz) sachet gelatine

1 punnet raspberries

1 tblspn raspberry liqueur

1 Beat cream with electric mixer until soft peaks form. Push mango through sieve to form a thick puree and fold into cream, stir in icing sugar.

2 Dissolve gelatine in ¼ cup cold water. Heat the gelatine gently until dissolved, stir into mango cream mixture. Pour mixture into ½ cup capacity moulds or ramekins, and chill until set.

3 Push raspberries through a sieve and stir in liqueur. Ease mousses out of moulds onto serving plates, serve with raspberry coulis.

Serves 4-6

Raspberry Cream Brulee

Raspberry Cream Brulee

4 egg yolks

1½ cups cream

1 cup tinned raspberries, drained

2 tblspn castor sugar

1 tspn vanilla essence

2 tblspn brown sugar

1 Beat egg yolks with castor sugar for 2 minutes. Scald the cream in a medium saucepan; slowly pour into egg mixture, whisking vigorously.

2 Add vanilla essence and return mixture to saucepan. Stir over low heat until thickened, without boiling. Remove from heat, cool, then refrigerate, stirring occasionally.

3 Divide raspberries between four heat-proof dishes (about ½ cup capacity). Pour chilled custard over each and sprinkle top with brown sugar.

4 Grill brulee for about 1 minute or until sugar has melted and begun to look like toffee. Serve immediately.

Serves 4

Hazelnut Ice Cream

90g (3oz) hazelnuts

1 cup cream

1 cup milk

½ cup sugar

1 tspn hazelnut liqueur (optional)

about ¼ tspn freshly squeezed lemon juice

1 Place hazelnuts on an oven tray, roast in the centre of a 180°C (350°F) oven until pale brown when peeled, about 12 minutes. Shake pan from time to time. Rub hazelnuts in a kitchen towel to remove skins.

2 Grind nuts in a processor for about 1 minute, stop once to scrape down sides of bowl.

3 Add cream, milk and sugar, process to blend. Add liqueur if used, and lemon juice to taste. Freeze in an ice cream maker according to manufacturer's instructions. Spoon into a container, keep frozen. When ready to eat, move to refrigerator for 10 minutes prior to serving.

Makes about 2½ cups

Poached Pears with Chocolate Sauce

3 cups sugar

2 tspn vanilla essence

4 firm pears, peeled

125g (4oz) dark chocolate, cut into 1cm (½in) cubes

¼ cup unsalted butter

¼ cup cream

1 Reserve 1 tablespoon of the sugar. Combine remaining sugar in a saucepan with 3 cups water. Stir over moderate heat until sugar has dissolved. Increase heat, boil 2 minutes. Reduce heat to low, add half the vanilla and the pears. Cover, poach pears until tender, about 25 minutes.

2 Remove pears from liquid, allow pears to cool. When liquid has slightly cooled, place in refrigerator.

3 Remove pear cores from the bottom, leave tops intact. Place in chilled liquid, keep refrigerated.

4 Combine chocolate, butter, cream and reserved sugar with ¼ cup water in a heavy saucepan. Bring slowly to a boil. Simmer until sauce is smooth and thickened, about 5 minutes. Add remaining teaspoon vanilla, remove from heat.

5 When ready to serve, remove pears from liquid, place in a serving dish. Drizzle with warm sauce, serve immediately.

Serves 4

Toasted Oats and Blackberry Coupe

1 cup rolled oats

1 cup cream, chilled

1 tblspn castor sugar

3 cups fresh blackberries, or frozen, defrosted

1 Place oats on a baking tray in an even layer. Toast in a 200°C (400°F) oven until golden, about 10 minutes. Shake tray from time to time. Pour onto a plate, cool.

2 In a bowl, beat cream until soft peaks form. Add sugar, beat until stiff peaks form. Fold oats into cream mixture.

3 Make layers of berries and cream in glass serving dishes, (large wine glasses are fine), begin with a layer of cream, end with a layer of berries. Serve at once.

Serves 4

Rich Chocolate Almond Dessert Cake

6 eggs, separated

¾ cup sugar

2 tblspn cocoa

100g (3½oz) blanched ground almonds

100g (3½oz) dark chocolate, melted

icing sugar to decorate

1 In a large bowl beat egg yolks with sugar until creamy. Beat in cocoa, almonds and melted chocolate; mixture will be very thick.

2 In a separate bowl, beat egg whites until fluffy. Fold egg whites into chocolate mixture.

3 Pour mixture into a 20cm (8in) cake tin lined with foil and greased well. Bake in moderate oven 35-40 minutes.

4 Remove from oven, let cool in tin for 10 minutes. Serve with cream and strawberries as desired, decorate with sifted icing sugar.

Serves 8

Apricots and Almonds

375g (¾lb) dried apricots

4 cups apple cider

60g (2oz) unsalted butter, cubed

¼ cup sugar

1 cup slivered almonds

1 Soak apricots in cider overnight.

Rich Chocolate Almond Dessert Cake (top); Cherry and Rhubarb Strudel

2 Place apricots and cider in a saucepan, bring to a boil over moderate heat, simmer, partially covered, until apricots are tender, about 10 minutes.

3 Remove pan from the heat, stir in butter and sugar. Continue stirring until butter is melted and sugar is dissolved. Cool.

4 Transfer apricots to a serving dish with a slotted spoon, strain syrup over apricots through a sieve, sprinkle with almonds. Serve chilled or at room temperature.

Serves 6

Cherry and Rhubarb Strudel

¾ cup stewed rhubarb

¾ cup tinned pitted cherries, drained

4 tblspn castor sugar

100g (3½oz) cake crumbs

1 sheet pre-rolled frozen puff pastry, thawed

1 cup whipped cream

1 In a medium saucepan, combine rhubarb, cherries and 2 tablespoons of the sugar. Cook over medium heat for 5 minutes; cool. Add cake crumbs to rhubarb and cherry mixture, mix well.

2 Place filling on top of pastry in a sausage shape and roll up in pastry, carefully tucking in ends as it is rolled.

3 Place strudel on a greased baking tray, with pastry join underneath. Sprinkle remaining sugar over top. Using a sharp knife, cut 2cm (¾in) slits along top of strudel.

4 Bake in moderate oven for 45 minutes or until pastry is golden. Serve with whipped cream.

Serves 4-6

Coffee Granita (top);
Hazelnut Cream Ice Cream

Ambrosia (top); Mixed Berry Mousse

Hazelnut Cream Ice Cream

2¼ cups milk

100g (3½oz) ground hazelnuts

1 cup cream

2 tblspn vanilla essence

6 eggs yolks

1 cup brown sugar

1 Bring milk to the boil in large saucepan. Add hazelnuts, cream and vanilla essence; reduce heat.

2 In a small bowl, beat egg yolks and sugar together with electric mixer until pale yellow. Slowly add 1 cup of milk mixture to egg and sugar mixture, while electric mixer is operating.

3 Add another cup of milk mixture to egg mixture while mixer is still operating. Pour combined egg and milk mixture into saucepan of remaining milk mixture and bring to the boil, stirring constantly, until mixture thickens.

4 Remove from heat, cool to room temperature. Pour mixture into a freezeproof container and freeze for 2 hours.

5 Remove from freezer, and whisk; return to freezer. Repeat Process after another 2 hours and then again after another 2 hours. Freeze until ready to serve.

Serves 6

Coffee Granita

½ cup sugar

3 cups strongly brewed black coffee

½ tspn cinnamon

½ tspn mixed spice

2 tblspn Tai Maria, or any coffee liqueur

mint to decorate

1 Place sugar, coffee, cinnamon, spice and Tia Maria in a saucepan; bring to the boil, boil for 2 minutes; cool.

2 Pour mixture into a freezeproof container and freeze for 3 hours. Remove from freezer and whisk mixture until ice has broken up.

3 Freeze another 3 hours, remove from freezer and whisk again. Return to freezer until ready to serve.

4 When ready to serve, remove from freezer and leave at room temperature for 15 minutes; then stir with a fork to crumble ice. Garnish with mint if desired.

Makes about 3 cups

Ambrosia

¾ cup tinned mandarin segments, drained

1 cup tinned pineapple pieces, drained

1 cup desiccated coconut

¼ cup walnut pieces

3 tblspn icing sugar

2 cups cream, whipped

1 Carefully fold mandarins, pineapple, coconut, walnuts and icing sugar into cream.

2 Divide mixture into 4 serving glasses. Serve chilled.

Serves 4

Mixed Berry Mousse

17g (¼oz) envelope of gelatine

2 tblspn framboise

2 tblspn icing sugar

1 cup mixed berries, drained

1½ cups cream, whipped

mint to decorate

1 Dissolve gelatine in ¼ cup cold water. In a large bowl gently mix together icing sugar, framboise and gelatine, add to the cream.

2 Fold berries carefully through cream mixture.

3 Divide mousse between 4 serving glasses and chill . Serve with mint to decorate.

Serves 4

TEMPERATURE AND MEASUREMENT EQUIVALENTS

OVEN TEMPERATURES

	Fahrenheit	Celsius
Very slow	250°	120°
Slow	275–300°	140–150°
Moderately slow	325°	160°
Moderate	350°	180°
Moderately hot	375°	190°
Hot	400–450°	200–230°
Very hot	475–500°	250–260°

CUP AND SPOON MEASURES

Measures given in our recipes refer to the standard metric cup and spoon sets approved by the Standards Association of Australia.

A basic metric cup set consists of 1 cup, ½ cup, ⅓ cup and ¼ cup sizes.

The basic spoon set comprises 1 tablespoon, 1 teaspoon, ½ teaspoon and ¼ teaspoon. These sets are available at leading department, kitchen and hardware stores.

IMPERIAL/METRIC CONVERSION CHART

MASS (WEIGHT)
(Approximate conversions for cookery purposes.)

Imperial	Metric	Imperial	Metric
½ oz	15 g	10 oz	315 g
1 oz	30 g	11 oz	345 g
2 oz	60 g	12 oz (¾ lb)	375 g
3 oz	90 g	13 oz	410 g
4 oz (¼ lb)	125 g	14 oz	440 g
5 oz	155 g	15 oz	470 g
6 oz	185 g	16 oz (1 lb)	500 g (0.5 kg)
7 oz	220 g	24 oz (1½ lb)	750 g
8 oz (½ lb)	250 g	32 oz (2 lb)	1000 g (1 kg)
9 oz	280 g	3 lb	1500 g (1.5 kg)

METRIC CUP AND SPOON SIZES

Cup	Spoon
¼ cup = 60 ml	¼ teaspoon = 1.25 ml
⅓ cup = 80 ml	½ teaspoon = 2.5 ml
½ cup = 125 ml	1 teaspoon = 5 ml
1 cup = 250 ml	1 tablespoon = 20 ml

LIQUIDS

Imperial	Cup*	Metric
1 fl oz		30 ml
2 fl oz	¼ cup	60 ml
3 fl oz		100 ml
4 fl oz	½ cup	125 ml

LIQUIDS (cont'd)

Imperial	Cup*	Metric
5 fl oz (¼ pint)		150 ml
6 fl oz	¾ cup	200 ml
8 fl oz	1 cup	250 ml
10 fl oz (½ pint)	1¼ cups	300 ml
12 fl oz	1½ cups	375 ml
14 fl oz	1¾ cups	425 ml
15 fl oz		475 ml
16 fl oz	2 cups	500 ml
20 fl oz (1 pint)	2½ cups	600 ml

* Cup measures are the same in Imperial and Metric.

LENGTH

Inches	Centimetres	Inches	Centimetres
¼	0.5	7	18
½	1	8	20
¾	2	9	23
1	2.5	10	25
1½	4	12	30
2	5	14	35
2½	6	16	40
3	8	18	45
4	10	20	50
6	15		

NB: 1 cm = 10 mm.